Use it or
Lose It!
How to keep your brain fit as it ages

Use it or
Lose It!
How to keep your brain fit as it ages

by

Allen D. Bragdon

and

David Gamon, Ph.D.

Allen D. Bragdon
Publishers, Inc.
CAPE COD & SAN FRANCISCO

Allen D. Bragdon Publishers, Inc.
252 Great Western Road
South Yarmouth, MA 02664

First Edition

The information in this book is intended to provide insight into how the brain functions. It is not intended for neurodiagnosis which must be conducted by qualified practitioners.

SCIENCE CONSULTANT: Suzanne Corkin, Ph.D., Professor of Behavioral Neuroscience, Department of Brain and Cognitive Sciences, Massachusetts Institute of Technology, Cambridge, MA

TECHNICAL EDITORS: Amanda Parker Ph.D., School of Psychology, University of Nottingham, United Kingdom

Cover design by Cindy Wood. Page Design and Editorial Production by Carolyn Zellers. Illustrations by Malcolm Wells. Index by Michael Loo.

Some images reproduced with permission of LifeArt Collection Images, copyright © 1989-99 TechPOOL Studios, Cleveland, OH; Puzzle graphics copyright © 2000 by Allen D. Bragdon Publishers, Inc.

Library of Congress Catalog Number: 00-191924

ISBN 0-916410-93-5

Printed in the United States of America

00 01 02 03   10 9 8 7 6 5 4 3 2 1

1. How Are You Doing? **9**
A SERIES OF TESTS OF MENTAL ACUITY
Including norms for scoring to determine if
there may be a problem

**2. Mental Lapses that You Don't Need to
   Worry About** **27**
SIGNS OF NORMAL, HEALTHY AGE-RELATED DECLINE
■ Divided attention tasks ■ Reaction time
■ Short-term recall ■ Naming ■ Proactive
inhibition

RESEARCH SHOWS THAT "USING IT PRESERVES IT"
■ Active older professors retain mental skills
that usually weaken with age

MAKING YOUR MEMORY WORK FOR YOU
■ Techniques for memorizing facts and for
retaining mental flexibility

**3. Common Cognitive Problems
   That Are Not Alzheimer's and
   What You Can Do About Them** **73**
EVALUATING THE SOURCES OF COGNITIVE
   PROBLEMS
■ Depression ■ Mini-strokes (TIAs) ■ Medication
■ Social isolation ■ Alcohol ■ Lifestyles without
challenge

COMMON SUBSTANCES THAT MAY HARM THE
BRAIN AND HOW YOU CAN COMBAT THEM
■ Cortisol ■ Free radicals ■ Beta-amyloid protein
■ "Killer" proteins

IF YOU DO HAVE ALZHEIMER'S
Current and future pharmaceutical therapies

**4. Preventing and Reversing Cognitive Decline
with Age Based on Current Research Results   97**

OUTMODED BELIEFS ABOUT THE BRAIN
■ Brain structure is fixed early in life ■ Brain cells don't
regenerate ■ Brain functions are strongly localized

NEW FINDINGS
■ The brain is a fluid system ■ Brain cells can
regenerate ■ Brain functions are widely distributed

PRACTICAL WAYS TO APPLY RESULTS
■ Intellectual challenge ■ Stimulating neurogenesis
by changing old patterns

COMMON SUBSTANCES IN THE BODY THAT MAY
HELP THE BRAIN AND HOW TO BOOST THEM
■ Stem cell research n Growth factors

**5. Conditioning Exercises Targeted to
the Specific Brain Functions that
Are at Risk with Aging   133**

Index   139

Solutions To Exercises   143

SECTION I

HOW ARE YOU DOING?

A SERIES OF TESTS OF MENTAL ACUITY

How are You Doing?

A Series of Tests of Mental Acuity

We are all aware of the problems faced by a graying society as the baby boomer demographic bulge moves towards retirement age. With the increasing numbers of old people, health care costs are starting to spiral and Social Security payments to balloon. One of the most prominent health care concerns these days is Alzheimer's Disease (AD). Just 30 years ago it was considered a rarity. Now, four million people have it in the U.S. alone. According to public health authorities, that translates into an annual financial burden of $100 billion. We can predict that, over the next 20 years, the numbers of people with the disease, and with it the financial burden, will go up by a factor of three.

On a more personal level, each one of us finds it unbearable that, simply by aging, we could lose our personality, our enjoyment of life, our memory, and ultimately our social acceptability. Fortunately, research into the biochemistry of aging and technology for manipulating that process are advancing rapidly. New technologies allow researchers to watch what parts of a living human brain are activated when its owner responds to test questions. Research results are accumulating daily identifying new roles for the brain's chemical messengers. We discover how identified groups of brain cells work together to process information. We uncover the actions of "stress" hormones, growth hormones, and other crucially important elements of the brain's complex and flexible support system.

It has become possible for scientists to identify specific genes that trigger memory storage, addiction, and other responses to the environment. These discoveries are being published in scientific journals today; they will change the way humans live in the next generation. But what can we do now? The baby boomer generation is turning 50 years old at the rate of six people per second as you read this. What can they do now to keep their lives interesting as their old age stretches out before them? How can they avoid losing their awareness of themselves and becoming an institutionalized burden on their families?

If you play with it, your mind will grow
Some of the most important research being conducted in universities and corporate laboratories these days is focusing on how to maintain the capacities of youth as the body ages. Research confirms that grandmother was right when she said that physical exercise is good for overall health. We now know that her advice applies to the mind as well as to the rest of the body: Those people who challenge their bodies and brains all their lives, will be more likely to benefit no matter how long they live.

Research with laboratory animals long ago showed that increasing mental activity also increased the size and quality of their brain cells. In those experiments researchers constantly changed the playthings in some of the mouse cages to challenge the animals in them to investigate and explore. Recent research confirms that forcing the mind to investigate and explore unfamiliar stimuli also improves performance in adult human brains. According to the most recent evidence, even high-tech, futuristic, invasive procedures such as fetal "stem" cell implants work better when they are used in a program of self-challenging, brain-stimulating lifestyle improvement.

Within this generation's lifetime, medical intervention may be able to improve memory, speed up mental reaction times, and lengthen concentration spans. But it will be expensive and, at least at first, will have unpredictable results and side effects from one individual to another. Right now there are ways to help maintain mental powers so that life will remain engaging as the years roll by.

What are the signs of Alzheimer's disease?
There is no test that can identify AD conclusively in a living human. Diagnosis can only be 100% certain after death. It takes an autopsy to reveal the characteristic plaques and tangles in the brain that are the sure sign of AD. While a person is still alive, a diagnosis of AD can be made with up to 90% accuracy by systematically using a battery of tests to rule out other possible causes of progressive cognitive decline one by one.

Should there be a personal reason to suspect dementia or reasons for a suspicion of its effects on the behavior of a friend or relative, make an appointment with a physician or psychologist trained in neurodiagnosis.

(Continued on page 18)

DSM-IV Diagnostic Criteria For AD

The standard diagnostic manual for mental disorders, the DSM-IV, cites the following criteria for dementia of the Alzheimer's type:

A. Development of multiple cognitive deficits:

  (1) memory impairment (learning new information or recalling previously learned information), and

  (2) one or more of the following:

   (a) language disturbance

   (b) difficulty carrying out motor activities (such as using a can opener, making the bed)

   (c) difficulty identifying objects

   (d) executive function difficulties (planning, organizing, abstracting).

B. The deficits in (A) cause impairment in work or social settings and represent a decline from a previous level.

C. The deficits begin gradually and continue to get worse.

D. The deficits are not due to other causes, such as stroke, brain tumor, Parkinson's, hypothyroidism, vitamin deficiency, HIV, prescription or over-the-counter drugs, or alcohol.

E. The deficits do not only occur during delirium.

F. The deficits are not better accounted for by another mental disorder, such as depression or schizophrenia.

(Source: American Psychiatric Association (1994). Diagnostic and Statistical Manual of Mental Disorders: DSM-IV. Washington, DC: American Psychiatric Association.)

A Short Mental Status Test

If you are worried about dementia, one of the first things to do is to get your physician, or a specialist recommended by your physician, to give you a preliminary mental status exam. This one is based on the Mini-Mental State Examination, designed by psychiatrists Folstein, Folstein, and McHugh in 1975, and still the most widely used preliminary screening test for dementia. This test is best done with two people, one to ask the questions and record the answers or point total. There is no time limit.

	Max Score	Score
		ORIENTATION
1)	5	What is the (1) date (2) year (3) day (4) month (5) season? (1 pt. each)
2)	5	Where are we? (If done at home) (1) state (2) county (3) town (4) street (5) house number (Adjust number 5 if not done at home.) (1 pt. each)
		REGISTRATION
3)	3	Examiner: Name three unrelated objects (e.g., chair, spoon, candlestick). Then, ask examinee to repeat them. (1 pt. for each object correctly repeated)
		ATTENTION AND CALCULATION
4)	5	Count backwards by sevens from 100 (93, 86, etc.). Stop after five answers. Or: Spell "world" backwards. (1 pt. each number or letter correct)
		RECALL
5)	3	What were the three objects mentioned in Question 3? (1 pt. each)

6) 2   LANGUAGE
         Examiner: Point to a pencil and a watch,
         and ask the examinee to name them.
         (1 pt. each)

7) 1   Repeat: "There's no such thing as a free
         lunch." (1 pt.)

8) 3   Follow this command: "Take a piece of
         paper, fold it in half, and put it on the
         floor." (1 pt. for each step)

9) 3   Read and follow these requests:
         (1) Point to your left ear
         (2) Write a sentence
         (3) Copy this design:
         (1 pt. each)

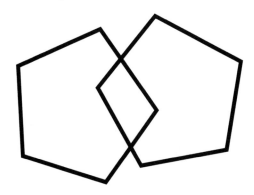

Scoring: A score of less than 25 means that cognitive impairment is likely — although not necessarily due to Alzheimer's — and that you should pursue further tests.

(Source: M.F. Folstein, S.E. Folstein, and P.R. McHugh (1975). Mini-mental state. Journal of Psychiatric Research 12: 189-98.)

A Quick Screening Exam:
The Time and Change Test

This is a recently-developed screening test for Alzheimer's and other dementias, created by researchers Froehlich, Robison, and Inouye. It has been shown to be very reliable in ruling out possible dementia, although very mild cases might still slip through.

TIME:
What time is it?
(Two tries allowed, maximum 1 minute.)

CHANGE:
    Select any coins that will add up to exactly one dollar. (2 tries allowed, maximum 2 minutes.)

Scoring: If either question cannot be answered correctly, there is possible dementia. If both questions are answered correctly, dementia is less likely.

(Source: T.F. Froehlich, J.T. Robison, and S.K. Inouye (1998). Screening for dementia in the outpatient setting: the Tine and Change Test. Journal of the American Geriatric Society 46:1506-11.)

Another Quick Screening Exam: The Set Test

This simple test for dementia, many variations of which are in use, was developed by psychiatrists Isaacs and Kennie in the early seventies. Like the Time and Change Test, it is very quick to take and easy to score.

For each of the following categories, allow 30 seconds to name as many items as you can (up to ten items per category):

(1) colors	(2) animals
(3) fruits	(4) towns

Scoring: 1 pt. for each correct item, for a maximum of 40 pts. total.
Less than 15: likely dementia, 15-24: possible dementia, 25+: no dementia

(Source: B. Isaacs and A.T. Kennie (1973). The Set Test as an aid to the detection of dementia in old people. British Journal of Psychiatry 123: 467-70.)

A Clinical Diagnosis of Probable AD Includes:

(1) Dementia established by a clinical exam and a mental status test such as the Mini-Mental State, and confirmed by neuropsychological tests;
(2) Deficits in at least two areas of cognition;
(3) Progressive worsening of memory and other cognitive abilities;
(4) No disturbance of consciousness;
(5) Onset between 40 and 90, usually after age 65;
(6) Absence of other disorders that could explain the dementia.

(Source: American Psychiatric Association (1994). Diagnostic and Statistical Manual of Mental Disorders: DSM-IV. Washington, DC: American Psychiatric Association.)

(Continued from page 12)

The physician will want details about the behaviors that raised the concern so make notes of specific changes in behavior and take them along. On the first visit some physicians prefer not to examine the subject but to interview only those people who have observed the patient closely, especially if they have done so over a long period of time. Close friends and family members will usually be more aware of, and more concerned about, memory lapses and signs of cognitive confusion than a person suffering from dementia.

The next step a physician or other professional advisor will take is to administer a mental status examination on the patient in order to get objective confirmation of cognitive difficulties, followed by physical and neurological examinations. Standard mental status examinations evaluate short-term memory, ability to pay attention to and follow simple directions, the ability to copy simple line drawings, and the like. In fact, the tasks in such standardized tests of mental status are so easy that difficulty answering even a small percentage of the questions indicates a likely cognitive problem.

If there is even suspicion of a problem
Because early symptoms of AD resemble standard signs of aging, they often go unnoticed. It is standard practice to take a complete medical history and to review the medical record for other possible causes of mental confusion that may be treated directly. Among the many causes of symptoms similar to those typical of dementia are side effects of prescription medications and over-the-counter medicine, vitamin deficiency, thy-

roid problems, alcohol abuse and diet. The symptoms of depression can mimic those of dementia. Depression is common among elderly people who may feel vulnerable, useless, lonely or embarrassed by physical or mental disabilities. Unlike dementia, however, depression is readily treated with lifestyle changes or medication.

If the results of the clinical examination test of mental status indicate a problem, the next step is to investigate the possibility of traumatic brain damage such as mini-strokes or a brain tumor. Eventually, if there is clear-cut cognitive decline and all the other possible causes have been ruled out, a tentative diagnosis of AD may be reached.

Warning signs

Often, symptoms that seem alarming signposts to dementia are typical of what is considered normal, healthy aging. All old people tend to experience memory loss or forgetfulness, occasional difficulty remembering a word or a name, and difficulty learning new tasks (how to use a personal computer, for example). Middle-aged and older people who are perfectly healthy may misinterpret insignificant mental lapses as dementia symptoms. A chart, on the following page, has been compiled by the Alzheimer's Association, to describe the most useful points of distinction between normal aging and dementia.

Age is the main risk factor

The single most important risk factor for AD is age. At age 65, only about two out of 100 people have serious mental disabilities that turn out to be AD. By age 80,

(Continued on page 22)

Normal Aging versus Dementia

Very early symptoms of progressive dementia, including AD, are mild — the sort of forgetfulness common among most older people, and even among some middle-aged ones. As the disease progresses, it becomes more easily distinguished from simple benign forgetfulness.

	Normal	Dementia
1) **Memory loss at work**	Occasionally forgetting an assignment, deadline, or colleague's name	Frequent forgetfulness and unexplainable confusion
2) **Difficulty with familiar tasks**	Occasional distractedness — forgetting to serve a dish that was intended to be included with a meal, for example	Severe forgetfulness — forgetting that you made a meal at all, for example
3) **Language impairment**	Occasional difficulty finding the right word	Frequent and severe difficulty finding the right word, resulting in speech that does not make sense
4) **Disorientation**	Occasionally forgetting the day of the week	Becoming lost on the way to the store
5) **Judgment problems**	Choosing an outfit that turns out to be somewhat warm or cold for the weather — neglecting to bring a sweater to a baseball game on a cool September evening, for example	Dressing blatantly inappropriately — for example, wearing several layers of warm clothing on a hot summer day

	Normal	Alzheimer's
6) Abstract think-ing difficulties	Occasional difficul-ty balancing a checkbook accu-rately	Inability to perform basic calculations, such as subtracting a check for $40 from a balance of $280
7) Misplacing objects	Misplacing keys or a wallet from time to time	Putting things in inappropriate places — a wallet in the oven, for example
8) Mood or behavior changes	Changes in mood from day to day	Rapid, dramatic mood swings with no apparent cause
9) Personality changes	Moderate person-ality change with age	Dramatic and dis-turbing personality change — for example, a tradi-tionally easygoing person becoming hostile or angry
10) Reduced initiative	Temporarily tiring of social obliga-tions or household chores	Permanent loss of interest in many or all social activities or chores

(Source: Alzheimer's Association Web site: www.alz.org.)

(Continued from page 19)

some current research shows that the ratio rises to at least 20 in 100 — one in five. By age 90, about half of all people have the disease. Four million older, adult Americans now have AD, and as the over-65 population increases over the next 20 years, the number is expected to triple.[1]

Genes

Neuroscientific research has revealed that there may be a genetic component to AD, though genetic predisposition is a much weaker risk factor than age. The fact that a parent or brother or sister has had AD does not mean that another sibling will end up getting it too. Genes play a more significant role in a small percentage of people who have the early-onset form of AD. About 40% of those people have a family history of the disease. Though this form is rare, it begins to show effects in middle age and progresses rapidly. Indeed, one of the reasons that nobody really heard much about Alzheimer's disease until about 30 years ago is that the early 20th-century pioneering research of Alois Alzheimer (after whom the disease is named) focused on the early-onset form. Until recently most people died before they could show the symptoms of the much more common late-onset type of AD. Those symptoms were typically viewed as just normal signs of aging, rather than as an expression of dementia.

The genetic contribution to some instances of late-onset AD is far weaker than for the early-onset version of the disease. Family history of AD is a far less important risk factor than age. The real danger, especially in the developed nations, is that when people retire they lose the incentive to exercise mentally and physically. Then, they must exert an increased effort to maintain mental and physical fitness in the absence of pressure from the demands of their job or stimulation from interactions with their peers. For them, it becomes all too easy to experience cognitive decline. And the catch is that then, year by year, they become increasingly susceptible to the cumulative causes of dementia wherever they come from.

Other risk factors

Only in recent years has the search for the causes — genetic and environmental — of AD intensified. The average life span in most developed nations is now over 70 and increasing. Until recently people did not live long enough to show the debilitating effects of dementia so seriously that those individuals required special care. However, there are countless millions of possible combinations of genetic and environmental factors. Despite intensive research it is still impossible to point to the causes of most mental deficits, much less correct them.

Many studies of identical twins prove that genes are not the whole story because even when both twins do get it, often many years intervene between onset in twin #1 and twin #2. With the common late-onset form, genetic risk is somewhat like the increased risk for skin cancer among people with blonde hair, blue eyes, and fair complexion.

Many variations in people's genetic inheritance may contribute to brain malfunction, including dementia. Environmental factors not related to genetic predisposition can play a role as well. Researchers are working hard to find out just what those factors are, so that the risk of AD can be reduced. Some of the following non-genetic factors may play a role.

Free radicals

Free radicals are highly reactive oxygen molecules created by our bodies as a natural by-product of using oxygen to convert our food into energy. What makes them so destructive to other cells and molecules in the body (including brain cells) is that they are unstable. The oxygen is primed to take part in a chemical reaction to produce energy so it will react with almost anything — including the surrounding tissue. Certain lifestyle factors, such as smoking or a high-fat diet, can increase the production of free radicals. Damage caused by excess free radicals may contribute to AD. The harmful effects of free radicals on the brain can be counteracted by other substances known as antioxidants. (See Chapter 3 for more about how raising levels of antioxidants may help protect cells in the brain.)

ENRICHED ENVIRONMENT # 207
A Gated Community

OK, so you don't test well. That doesn't mean you aren't a really, really nice mouse who's welcome here.

Enriched environment and mood

The term "enriched environment" refers to a lifestyle that enjoys an adequate level of physical, mental, and social activity. Many studies have have produced evidence that maintaining an active lifestyle in all three of these domains not only stimulates the brain, but helps to keep the brain's neurons alive and healthy. It also protects brain cells from damage. Physical and mental activity boost production of the brain's own maintenance-and-repair systems including brain-protective chemicals known as growth hormones. Activity also increases the survival rate of newly-generated brain that could help slow down the effects of AD.

A high-stress lifestyle raises levels of stress hormones, which in turn destroy brain cells. Depression, too, can contribute to cognitive decline. This set of factors is not completely separate from the environmental-enrichment ones because physical, mental, and social stimulation improve mood and alleviate depression as well as providing more direct benefits to the brain. (See the following chapters for further details and supportive evidence.)

The importance of these and other non-genetic factors is that they can play a crucial role in improving the quality of life by motivating people to maintain their brains in a fit and healthy condition regardless of any possible genetic predisposition to developing AD. Many aspects of normal, healthy aging — poorer memory, reduced problem-solving ability, slower acquisition of new facts and skills — can be helped by lifestyle changes.

FOOTNOTES FOR SECTION I

[1] Mayo Clinic Web site: www.mayohealth.org.

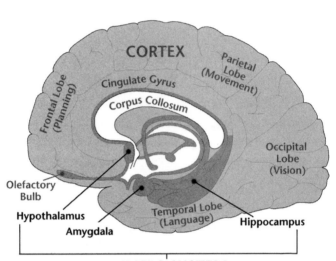

CORTEX

Parietal Lobe (Movement)

Cingulate Gyrus

Corpus Collosum

Frontal Lobe (Planning)

Occipital Lobe (Vision)

Olefactory Bulb

Hypothalamus

Amygdala

Temporal Lobe (Language)

Hippocampus

LIMBIC SYSTEM

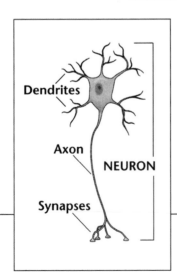

Dendrites

Axon

NEURON

Synapses

The diagram, above, shows the brain's interior with the "gray matter" of the thinking cortex atop the more primitive limbic system, which controls instinctive responses, emotions and memory.

At left, a diagram of a common type of brain cell. Electro-chemical impulses travel down the axon through the synapses to the dendrites of adjacent cells This causes them to fire impulses to other cells.

MENTAL LAPSES THAT YOU *DON'T* NEED TO WORRY ABOUT

SIGNS OF NORMAL, HEALTHY AGE-RELATED DECLINE

RESEARCH PROVES THAT "USING IT PRESERVES IT"

MAKING YOUR MEMORY WORK FOR YOU

Mental Lapses That You *Don't* Need To Worry About

Signs of Normal, Healthy Age-Related Decline

Everybody knows that some aspects of our bodies and minds change as we get older. If a professional baseball player who just turned 40 cannot get his bat around on a fastball as quickly as he could at age 20, nobody thinks that anything is amiss. Slower reaction times are one of the changes we accept as part of aging. We compensate for age-related changes with a greater depth of experience, which we apply to the decisions that we make.

Are changes in our mental abilities natural signs of aging? Will memory skills become weaker as we get older? Learning skills? Mental quickness? Intellectual stamina? Are we likely to forget names more often? Are such changes signs that something is going wrong?

About 47% of older adults over 80 will develop AD (or dementia), and there is enormous variability in the "normal" or "acceptable" age-related changes shown by people who do *not* develop the disease. Some 80-year-olds show obvious deterioration in mental agility without necessarily being classified as demented. Other 80-year-olds show little change at all. So should we accept the "acceptable" changes after all? We need to to ask why some people change more than others, and to ask ourselves what we can do about it.

Reaction time

With the brain, as with the body, one of the most obvious age-related changes is a slowing down in reaction
time, the time it takes a person to respond to an event.
Older people generally perform worse on tasks that are
"against the clock."[1,2] They need more time to perform
multi-step tasks, both physical and mental.

One of the reasons driving skill tends to fall off in old
age is that reaction time slows down. This slowing
affects simple and more complex forms of response to
events. An example of simple reaction time is a need
quickly to apply the brakes or turn the wheel if a dog
runs into the road. Deciding whether an upcoming
freeway exit is the correct one to take is an example of
a more complex decision that need fast reaction time

The fact that reaction time almost invariably and
inevitably slows with age does not mean that overall
performance will be worse on all cognitive tasks. Just as
the aging baseball player can draw on his greater experience to anticipate the need for a specific response,
older people have an accumulation of wisdom and
experience that can compensate for a slower brain.
After all, the reason young people are bad insurance
risks — despite their good reflexes and mental speed —
is that they have more accidents. They make mistakes
because they are inexperienced and sometimes reckless.

When age puts a damper on all mental processing the
overall result may be that an older person takes longer
to arrive at a correct solution. In fact, some researchers
believe that a general slowing of mental function lies at
the base of all normal age-related cognitive decline.[3]

They speculate that slowed mental processes are due to an overall reduction in the efficiency of brain cells They propose that a drop in mental processing performance with age cannot be just a matter of slower physical reaction time. Evidence for this claim is that, in simple reaction time tasks, the difference between young and older people is far less than it is for more complex or demanding tasks.[4,5] Therefore, slower response shows up in thinking speed, not just physical response.

Older people tend to perform worse on a variety of memory-related tasks, even when they are not under time pressure. For example, they tend to have more difficulty remembering the details of a newspaper article than younger adults do. Some researchers propose that slower processing speed lies at the root of the typical, age-related drop in memory skills.[6,7,8] They say that because new information is being processed more slowly as it comes in, the memory traces of one piece of information have begun to decay before the next piece of information is received. The brain cannot reach back to combine the pieces into a meaningful, coherent whole, which is essential to remembering details. We do not yet know whether this kind of memory problem a result of slower processing or even if it should be accepted as inevitable and "natural." Some interesting research shows that, in fact, many such "normal" signs of aging can be prevented by exercising the mind in certain ways.

A Skill That Does Not Decline
With Age: Vocabulary

Every one of these adjectives relates to an animal. Which animal? (They get harder farther down the list.)

1. feline
2. canine
3. equine
4. leonine
5. porcine

6. piscine
7. lupine
8. bovine
9. aquiline
10. phocine

(Hint: In Nabokov's novel *Lolita*, the narrator Humbert refers to Lolita's mother, lounging by the swimming pool in a black one-piece, as "her *phocine* mama."

Scoring:

5 = average   6 = good   7= very good

8 = excellent   9-10 = outstanding

Memory: Many skills with one name

To understand how memory fails it helps to know how it works. A wide variety of impulses can trigger the brain to commit an event to memory. A strong emotion can do it, so can boring repetition, but the key to building memory-power that lasts is to be able to associate a new fact with one the brain has already stored. Then the brain can say, "oh yes, *this* is like *that*." The more a brain has learned, the more new stuff it can remember. The brain uses different circuits to commit different categories of data to memory. It handles how to ride a bike differently from recalling how a favorite wine smells or where the car keys are at the moment.

The short and the long of it

What we loosely refer to as "memory" is, in fact, many different processes that occur in different parts of the brain. Most of us are already familiar with the basic distinction between short-term memory and long-term memory. These are fundamentally different, albeit interacting, processes. Only a small fraction of short-term memories get converted into long-term storage. When the brain creates long-term memories, it synthesizes protein for new dendrites and axon pathways, after deciding whether an event it is experiencing is important enough to retain. In other words, only long-term memories depend on structural changes in the brain.[9] Short-term memories exist in the cortex; conversion of short- into long-term memories requires the assistance of the *hippocampus* — a curved structure within the brain — but once memories are consolidated into long-term storage by repeated rehearsal, the hippocampus plays a less and less important role in retrieving them.

The long-term memories themselves are housed in many regions of the cortex, often corresponding to the part of the brain that became activated during the initial experience of the event or fact. In this sense, there is no one "memory" region of the brain. The brain even stores the names of different categories of objects in different places. Faces are stored separately from foods; tools separately from animals, for example.[10]

What is happening, or not, in the brain

The kinds of memory loss that happen as we age can be understood in terms of changes in certain structures in the brain. Two areas in the brain that suffer decline in even healthy older people are the hippocampus and the

frontal lobes.[11,12] The hippocampus is a structure within
the brain that plays a crucial role in processing incom-
ing information and creating long-term memories out
of them, and (to varying degrees) in retrieving memories from storage sites scattered widely throughout the
cortex. The frontal lobes play a role in devising strategies for organizing and memorizing new information, in
effortful attempts to retrieve that information from
memory, and in remembering the source of the information. This last aspect of memory is called *source
memory*; a failure in source memory reveals itself when-
ever we recall something that someone told us without
remembering who told us, or when, or where, or why.
Source memory is a problem especially for children,
whose frontal lobes have not yet developed fully, as well
as for older adults, whose frontal lobes may have lost a
sizeable fraction of their mass.[13,14] Frontal-lobe-based
memory failure may also show itself as a tendency to
forget to follow through on plans — a problem, once
again, common to young children and older adults
alike.

Working memory and executive skills
Working memory (which the scientific community short-
ens to "WM") is the ability to keep information in mind
while the brain manipulates it in some way, a task that
commonly becomes more difficult with aging. For example, to multiply 7 X 13 in one's head, the brain must
remember the numbers involved — 7 and 13 — and then
perform an operation — multiplication — on them. First
the brain must break the problem down into 7 X 10, plus
7 X 3. Then, the brain must remember what it has
accomplished at each step, as it proceeds to further steps.

Another test of WM skills that psychologists use is to ask the subject to listen to a list of numbers, then repeat them back in reverse order. To complete the task successfully all the numbers, individually, must be retained "on line," then rearranged. This combination of short-term memory and on-line monitoring and manipulation is a demonstration of WM at work.

Closely related to WM are *executive skills*. These uniquely human skills help to select goals, devise strategies to attain those goals, and monitor progress toward implement those strategies. The goals can be as simple as working out the right order in which to do all the tasks necessary to cook a meal, or as complex as attaining a college degree. Executive skills are considered a "higher-order," recently evolved aspect of human intelligence. Even though executive ability applies to skills other than memory, it is clear that the on-line monitoring and manipulation of data involved in WM depends on well-functioning executive skills. In fact, whether a person's WM is good or bad may depend on how well or poorly her executive skills are functioning.[15,16,17]

Executive and WM faculties typically weaken with age. Another type of working memory test that psychologists use involves a grid of patterns like that shown here. The subject, seated in front of a computer screen with this series of patterns on it, is asked to point to any one of the patterns in the grid. As soon as he does this, a different screen appears with all the same patterns in *different* locations. Now, he has to point to any one of the patterns *except* the one he already pointed to on the first screen. And so it continues, with the patterns appearing in a different configuration each time. The subject's task is always to point to any pattern that he had not already pointed to before.

This task is difficult because it places a burden on short-term memory, and also challenges executive skills. Short-term memory must load and recall every pattern that has been selected, then identify the ones that have not been selected before by pointing to them. Obviously, part of the brain's task is to devise strategies that will minimize the chance of making an error.

People whose frontal brain lobes have been injured have a particularly hard time on tests like this.[18] Typically they may have suffered a stroke or tumor in the front of their brain or a blow to the front part of their skull. (Remarkably, some people with frontal lobe damage may even *know* that they are making the wrong choice on a task like this, but be unable or unwilling to control their behavior.[19])

Older people also perform worse than average on tests of executive skills, which suggests that working memory, and particularly executive ability, tends to deteriorate with age.[20,21,22] A likely cause is that cells in the frontal lobes of the cortex tend to atrophy during aging more than most other parts of the brain.[23,24] To measure working memory and executive function psychologists also use other tests. An ability to follow complex sentences also measures key memory functions (see "Memory Span Test," opposite) and is more like real life.

Memory interference

Executive skills are a general faculty that helps organize and monitor other, more specific, mental abilities like attention, memory, and language. One of the skills that is important in trying to solve a problem or attain a goal is to know what information *is not* useful. For example, to test the validity of a claim that "all swans are white," which would be a more crucial piece of data: A black swan, or a white one? The correct answer is the black swan, since even a single example of a black variety disproves the claim that all swans are white. A white swan, on the other hand, can neither prove nor disprove the claim, so a white one is not really relevant. This kind of mental self-control — separating the important information from the unimportant, and leaving a piece of information out of consideration if it does not really help solve the problem — is a skill that we cultivate carefully in school, and that we tend to lose to some degree as we get old.

One important way that irrelevant information can impact memory performance has been called *interference* by psychologists. Suppose that someone bought a short story anthology, and read two of the stories in one sitting. In this case, it would be harder to remember all the details of both stories as well as if the reader had waited a few hours or days before reading the second one. This loss is due to interference. Memory of one story interferes with long-term memory of the other. If the first one blots out the second, that is called *proactive* interference; if the sec-

---

Memory Span Test

An important skill required for effective working memory is the ability to store information temporarily and then refer back to it on demand. This test demonstrates that ability.

(1) Read the following sentence aloud, then turn to page 38 and answer the question printed in the left margin.

"The bus driver motioned the red truck to continue, which turned left, stopped by the third driveway, and sounded its horn twice."

(2) Read the following sentence. Then try to answer the questions in the right margin of page 39:

"The acrobat discussed game theory with a trained harbor seal riding on a tiger in a wagon pulled by a white stallion."

---

ond interferes with recalling the first one well, that is *retroactive* interference. Here is a common example of retroactive interference: A person thinks of something that needs attention in another room then rises and goes there. On the way, because of something seen or heard, another task comes to mind. "Why," the person wonders, "did I come into this room?" Interference disrupts memory for all kinds of things at all ages, from stories to the score of a tennis game to people's names. However, it is one of the memory-related problems that tends to get worse as people age. In particular, proactive interference — the way that something learned at 2:00 interferes with the memorization of something encountered at 3:00 — affects older people more strongly than younger people.[25,26]

Divided attention
Older people may also have problems following conversations in noisy environments. In this case, irrelevant

From page 37, #1: What direction did the truck turn?

information is affecting their attention to a task, which may have something to do with the kind of mental self-control provided by executive skills. Anyone who has ever tried to follow the dialog of a television program, while someone in the same room is talking about something interesting, knows how hard it can be to pay attention to two things at once. This kind of problem comes up in social situations when several people are talking at once. When older people tend to have difficulty pulling apart several threads of conversation, it may be partly a matter of hearing loss, but there is usually more to it.

Scientists test people's ability to keep track of two simultaneous streams of information using *divided attention tasks*. In these tasks, the subjects wear headphones, with, say, one series of numbers coming into the left headphone and a different series coming into the right. Then, the subjects have to repeat the two series, without mixing up the numbers from one series with the other. On this kind of task, older people tend to perform worse than younger people.

Slowest to develop, and quickest to fade: Frontal-lobe skills

All these findings suggest that some mental abilities, especially memory, will be affected by age-related changes. This result can be expected as a normal part of aging. An overall increase in the time needed to figure things out or to solve problems is normal. It is also typical for older people to have a harder time keeping something in their mind — say, a telephone number — long enough to perform some task with it — say, dial it. It also gets harder to organize information efficiently, to sort out the relevant from the irrelevant, and to keep the memory of one piece of information from interfering with another. Most, if not all, of these skills center on the brain's frontal lobes, the region of the brain that is slowest to develop as we grow up.[27,28] The frontal lobes house skills which tend to be complex and effortful, the kind of learning skills we need to practice (in school and afterwards) in order for them to become and remain sharp. In this sense, frontal-lobe skills are ones that come the least naturally to us. The frontal lobes are the quickest to deteriorate with age so they tend to lose the most capacity. Their reduced mass is caused mostly by loss of "white matter" *glial* cells which provide connections between the neurons that make up the "grey matter" of the cortex. All these changes are part of normal aging, *not* signs of dementia. They show up as changes in capacity, just as, say, the gradual deterioration of muscle tone saps physical strength. A significant reason some people's mental skills seem to suffer less than others is that people who continue to put demands on their brain cells force the brain to recruit idle cells that have not yet been seriously affected by the aging process.

From page 37, #2: What theory did the seal discuss? What were the last words of the two sentences on page 37?

RESEARCH PROVES THAT "USING IT PRESERVES IT"

Mental slowdown is normal...but not necessarily inevitable: What a study of 72 Berkeley professors tells about successful aging

There is compelling evidence, though, that these problem-solving and memory skills do not have to get worse with age, even though they may require more effort to keep them working well. A few years ago, the cognitive performance of 72 professors teaching at the University of California, Berkeley, was tested.[29] The results showed that working memory and executive skills may be affected by the degree to which people challenge themselves mentally as they age.

The study tested the cognitive skills of five groups of people: Young non-professors, old non-professors, and younger, middle-aged, and older professors. The mental abilities tested were reaction time, working memory, prose recall, and something called *paired associate learning,* which is the memorization of arbitrary pairs, such as names and faces. (See box, opposite.) The non-professors showed the typical age-related decline in all these cognitive skills: The younger people performed significantly better than the older ones.

(Continued on page 42)

A Skill That Declines With Age, No Matter How Sharp You Keep Your Mind: Paired Associate Learning

Paired associate learning means the memorization of arbitrary pairs (faces, names, and so forth). Healthy older people naturally perform worse on this kind of task than their younger counterparts, even if they have kept themselves mentally fit. The problem with paired associate learning is that the pairs are arbitrary, and do not fit into any kind of pre-existing knowledge base. In order to memorize the pairs, you have to apply some sort of mnemonic trick or other, a frontal-lobe-based technique that apparently comes less automatically to you as you get older.

You will need a timer. Your task is to remember which female face goes with which male face. Study the six pairs of faces on this page for four seconds each (24 seconds total), and then continue to the instructions below.

Next, look at the box of six male faces on page 43. Match each male face to one of the female faces in the box below, following the pairings on this page to the best of your recollection. Do not spend longer than a minute. (On these quick timed tasks, ask a friend to time you so you are not preoccupied with the stopwatch.) Repeat the task twice, observing the same time limits.

(Continued from page 40)

Visual WM

Among the professors, however, the results were different. The older professors (ages 60-71) did show the typical declines in the reaction time and paired associate learning tests compared to middle-aged (45-59) and younger (30-44) professors.

On other tests, the older professors' performance was more interesting. Imagine being given this task: (See page 34).The professor taking the test (the "subject") is shown 16 patterns in a grid and asked to select just one. Then the subject is shown the same patterns but arranged in a different way and asked to pick any single grid that is *different* from the first one picked, and so on. After seeing 16 pattern-grids in succession, the subject is taken through a second trial with the same patterns, and with the same instructions. This procedure places a greater burden on short-term memory skills since the subject has to separate the patterns picked on the first trial from the patterns picked in a previous turn on the second trial. All the selections made on the first trial should be regarded as irrelevant to the choices made on the second, but it is easy to get confused.

Essentially, this task is designed to show up proactive interference confusion. Earlier-remembered patterns interfere with the ability to remember or keep track of similar patterns encountered later in the test. As we already explained, older people tend to have a harder time with this than younger people. For this

(Continued on page 46)

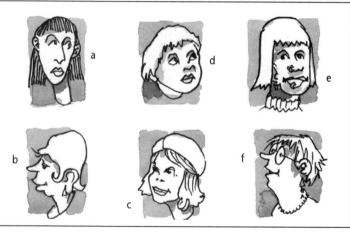

Norms:

    First trial: Two correct for older subjects (60-71 years), three correct for younger subjects (18-23 years)

    Second trial: Two correct for older subjects, four correct for younger subjects

    Third trial: Three correct for older subjects, five correct for younger subjects

1___
2___
3___
4___
5___
6___

Trail Making Test

The Trail Making Test is a test of complex visual scanning, attention, mental flexibility, and motor speed. It can be used to help verify head trauma or dementia, but even among normal, healthy people performance on the test tends to decline dramatically with age. This is a timed test, so you will need a clock, watch, or stopwatch.

Instructions: On the opposite page are some letters and numbers. Begin at letter A ("start"), and draw a line from A to 1, 1 to B, B to 2, and so on, in order until you reach the last number ("end"). Note the time taken to complete the entire series.

Norms: The time taken to complete this test varies with age as well as with education level. For example, the average healthy 15-to-20-year-old needs 47 seconds to finish the trail, while the average healthy 70-to-79-year-old needs 180 seconds. Normal adults 40-60 years old with less than 12 years of education need 102 seconds, while those with at least 16 years of education need a little less than one minute. The following table shows the norms by age group. You can see how large the range is even among healthy, non-demented adults.

Trail Making Test: Time in Seconds Needed by Healthy Subjects to Complete, by Age

Percentile	15-20	20-39	40-49	50-59	60-69	70-79
90	26	45	30	55	62	79
75	37	55	52	71	83	122
50	47	65	78	80	95	180
25	59	85	102	128	142	210
10	70	98	126	162	174	350

(Note: A score in the 90th percentile means 90% of people in that age group score lower, etc.)

(Source: U.S. Army Individual Test Battery)

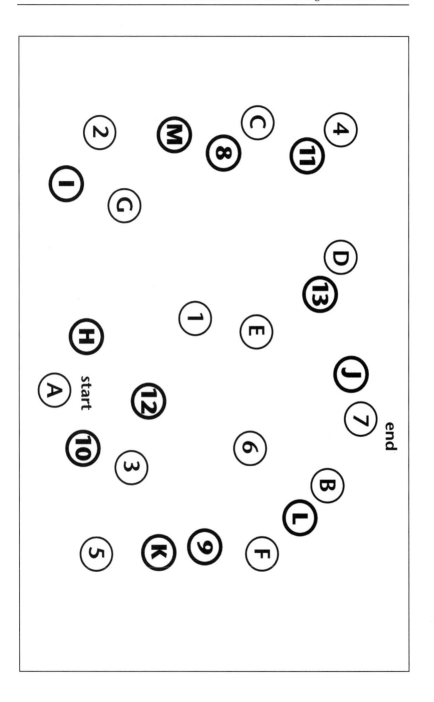

Recognition vs. Recollection List #1

Take a minute to memorize the items on this shopping list. Then cover the list and write down as many items as you can recall. Next, turn the page and look at List #2 there. It contains some of the items listed below. Which ones? Which was easier? Moral: Recognition is easier than recollection, especially when you get older.

Milk	Tomatoes
Eggs	Soup
Lettuce	Carrots
Onions	Swiss cheese
Mayonnaise	Yogurt
Ice cream	Apples
Green beans	Peanut Butter
Ham	Margarine
Ketchup	Ground beef
Salt	Broccoli

(Continued from page 42)

experiment, the group of older non-professors did indeed make more mistakes in the second run-through of the task than the first. In this way they showed the typical age-related vulnerability to proactive interference. The older professors, on the other hand, made fewer mistakes in the second trial. This pattern was shared with the young and middle-aged professors and with the group of young non-professors. In other words, the older professors showed none of the normal increase in proactive interference with age.

The same pattern arose in the prose recall test. In the

general population, older people do worse than younger people when they have to remember details from a passage that has just been read to them. Among the professors, on the other hand, there were no age differences in performance: Older professors did just as well as, or even better than, young ones.

These findings indicate there is not need to accept all of the kinds of cognitive loss considered "inevitable" as we get older. The older professors sustained a high level of activity in grappling with conceptually challenging material. This was probably because of their job requirements and their interests. Despite the fact that retention of the details of a prose passage is considered to be a highly age-sensitive test, older professors could remember just as many details as young ones. And in the working memory test, older professors demonstrated just as much mental self-control as younger ones in keeping their choices in successive trials of the pattern-picking test from interfering with one another. It may be, then, that the daily practice these senior professors have in acquiring and organizing new knowledge helps them to perform well on these tasks.

Where the older professors faltered

Tests the older professors did not do as well on as the younger professors may give us some insight into mental abilities that inevitably deteriorate with age, and how the older professors got around these deficits. Why would intellectual exercise not have a protective effect against poorer performance in tests of reaction time and paired associate learning?

As the authors of the study point out, an obvious answer is that reaction time and paired associate learning abilities have relatively little impact on the conceptual skills that the older professors use on a daily basis. Many of the tests we have been discussing, which psychologists use to evaluate the memory skills of all kinds of people, are rather arbitrary and divorced from real life. Simply memorizing associations between pairs of names, for example, or memorizing a list of name-face pairs, has little to do with how people normally integrate new information with pre-existing knowledge. This conclusion also applies to other standard tests of short-term memory, such as memorizing a string of randomly-chosen numbers. Reaction time, too, has little to do with conceptual knowledge.

Older people generally have a harder time with high-level planning, organizing, and problem-solving skills than do younger people. For example, trying to coordinate a dinner party so that the date and time will be most convenient for as many of the guests as possible will require juggling a lot of information about the guests and their different sets of priorities. This task is harder at age 70 than at age 30. These quintessentially human executive skills, remember, are housed in the brain's frontal lobes, which suffer a significant drop in blood flow and energy use with age.[30,31] So the daily intellectual exercise of the older professors may either have a protective effect against frontal-lobe deterioration, or give them strategies to overcome this deterioration, just as an older baseball player can develop strategies to compensate for slower reflexes.

Memory and executive skills
Many other experiments have documented mental skills that depend on executive and planning functions

that tend to decline as we age.[32] If you show older people a shopping list, and ask them a few seconds or minutes later what was on the list, they will tend to have a harder time than younger people remembering what items were there. But if shown a second list that includes some items from the first list mixed in with some new items, they will not have as much difficulty picking out the items they saw on the original list.[33,34] In other words, their *recognition* is better than their *recollection*. Recollection, therefore, is the retrieval of a piece of information from memory without any external cue to help the process along. Although recollection often seems to be a simple and effortless task, it is heavily dependent on executive skills.

Recollection is important in everyday life and losing it leads to embarrassment when, for example, a person

---

Recognition vs. Recollection List #2

Look at the grocery list below. It contains some of the items included in List #1 on page 46. Which ones? Which was easier?

Cream	Bread
Eggs	Soup
Lettuce	Peppers
Onions	Swiss cheese
Mustard	Yogurt
Ice cream	Apples
Spinach	Peanut Butter
Ham	Margarine
Olives	Ground beef
Salt	Broccoli

finds himself shopping and cannot remember what was needed at the grocery store, or what a friend's baby granddaughter's name is. Tasks like these require effortful strategies by the brain's frontal region to recover that piece of information from memory. In social situations the penalty for forgetting a name is unnerving. The fear of failing to come up with someone's name causes the brain to close down the circuits that could assemble the components of memory needed to produce the name. In that situation the problem is fear of social embarrassment, not dementia.

Fortunately, it is easy to remember something that *does not* require an effortful retrieval strategy, like whether one has seen a certain name before. The same is true in recalling familiar facts, such as the name of a family member. In tasks like these, the frontal lobes participate less, and older and younger people perform more or less equally well.

Brain function can be studied with a PET scanner, which produces images of which parts of a person's brain are active during different sorts of mental tasks. Experiments using PET have shown that the frontal lobes of older people are not only less active while they are trying to retrieve a fact from memory, but also while they are trying to *encode* a fact or detail.[35,36] Encoding is the process of laying down a memory trace in the brain by changing some of the neurons. For an example of the type of task that is used in these experiments, take a look at the collection of faces opposite. Study them carefully enough to feel confident of remembering what they look like a minute or so from now. After studying them, continue reading.

Different kinds of memory-related tasks impose different demands on the brain. Drawing one of the faces in the box above from memory uses the brain's executive skills to aid the process of recollection. Performing this task efficiently requires the kind of mental effort that would reveal itself, in a PET scan, in increased activity in the frontal lobes. Some people are better at this kind of memory task than others, which is reflected in the fact that some people's brains show a lot more frontal-lobe activity than others. Generally, older people show less frontal-lobe activity than younger people, and perform less well on this kind of memory task — evidence that mental effort to retrieve information from memory is related to activity in the frontal lobes.

Tricks to help an imperfect memory
Because memory is not a single mental ability, we can benefit from a range of tricks that help us to remember more efficiently. First, consider that some memory tasks require less effort from the frontal lobes than others. Take a look at the face shown above, left. Do not look back at the box of faces on the previous page. Was this face in that box? You will recall from the discussion above that answering this question is easier for young and old people because it is a recognition test, which places a smaller burden on your frontal lobes. People vary a lot, on the other hand, in how hard their frontal lobes work when they are studying or *encoding* the faces in the first place. Younger people tend to show more frontal lobe activity than older people. This region of the brain plays an important role in what is called *elaborative* encoding. In other words, the kind of memorization strategy called elaborative encoding happens more vigorously in younger adults than older ones. What, then, is elaborative encoding? And can older people develop their skills in elaborative encoding by deliberately using elaborative techniques?

cat	chair	cup	rose
shirt	grass	ball	door

Take a look at the word-list in the box above. As an aid to help memorize the words on this list, consider such questions as, "Is a *shirt* a kind of clothing?" Answering this question propels thinking about what the word means, which helps fix it in memory. On the other hand,

the question, "How many vowels are in the word *shirt*?"
would not help recall of the word a few minutes later.
The first question is an example of *elaborative* encoding,
which means integrating the new fact into existing
knowledge, to make it more meaningful. Information
that is meaningful (as opposed to just random or arbitrary, such as a string of random numbers) is easier to
remember.

What this means, then, is that it is less natural for an older
person to make the mental effort to elaborate memories as
they are encoded. This lack of effort is bad for memory
because it is the effort of elaboration that will help recall
of a detail a few minutes or days down the road. Just
because it comes less naturally, however, does not mean it
cannot be done. In fact, many of the conscious *mnemonic*
tricks people use to help them remember things use elaboration. These tricks can serve to compensate when memory is not elaborating as automatically and efficiently as it
could be made to.

Try this trick: Someone drives to the airport to pick up a
friend. The airport garage is so large it is divided up into
different sections, each labeled with a letter-number combination. It will be hard to recall the arbitrary location
code unless an effort is made to make it meaningful so as
to *encode* the location in memory. For example, to convert
a letter-number combination, say C-2, into something
easier to remember, picture returning to the lot with the
friend, who says, "I *see* it *too*" when the car is located.
Combining a random letter-number with a visual image,
is a huge help. (Tip: He who writes the location code on a
garage parking ticket must *not* leave the ticket in the car!)

Self test: How to Remember People's Names

Learning personal names is an ability that appears to vary considerably across individuals, and forgetting names is the most frequent memory complaint among the elderly. Even poor name memorizers, however, can overcome this deficit through the use of simple mnemonic tricks based on an understanding that when information is encoded in a personally *meaningful* way (which is sometimes referred to as the memorization being more "elaborated"), the more likely memory is to be enhanced.

A. Miller

A. Roundy

C. Bins

J. Richardson

For each of the above face-name pairings:
1) Identify a prominent facial feature.
2) Transform the person's name into a concrete, visually vivid object.
3) Mentally picture the facial feature combined with the transformed name-object.

(Examples: A man with long hair named O'Brien; transform "O'Brien" to "lion," and visualize a lion's mane emerging from his head. A woman with heavy eyebrows named Crocker; transform "Crocker" to "cracker," and visualize a cracker on her eyebrows.) This technique can be further strengthened by performing the final step of making an *emotional* judgment of the pleasantness or unpleasantness of the image association.

Anybody can use techniques like this to help memory as a practical matter. PET scan studies of young and old people show that older subjects might need to rely on memory aids more than younger ones because elaborative encoding strategies come less *automatically* to most brains as they age.[37] That change does not necessarily mean that younger adults are unconsciously applying any particular trick that we may be able to use in a learned mnemonic strategy. They may, for example, be more efficient in filing into memory a series of a visual "snapshots" along the path they followed from the location. Consciously or not, at age 30, people certainly make more efficient initial encoding efforts than they do at age 70.

Mnemonic tricks, or memory aids, are not really things that strengthen the power of memory, but they do help compensate for a less-than-perfect memory. The results from the U.C. Berkeley study of professors extend this conclusion to older people who exercise their memory a lot. The older professors were very good at prose recall, where they had to remember facts from a meaningful passage. On the other hand, they were not as good at paired associate learning, where they had to memorize arbitrary face-name pairs. This means that even healthy, active 70-year-olds will need to use memory crutches if they want to memorize arbitrary details. A very simple trick for remembering where you left your car key, for example, might be to put it in the exact same place every time you set it down. There is nothing wrong with relying on a strategy like this, and it definitely does *not* signal dementia.

MAKING YOUR MEMORY WORK FOR YOU

The tests that psychologists use to gauge cognitive abilities are, like almost all psychological and scholastic aptitude tests, standardized. They assume that all people, or all people of a certain age, should perform within a certain range in order to be "normal" or "average." The reasons one person performs worse than another may have nothing to do with age-related cognitive decline, or even poor overall cognitive fitness. Everybody's brain works differently, and nobody — not even a certified genius — is good at all tasks. The human brain comes equipped with a variety of mental abilities, Even though they often support and interact with each other, every brain ends up demonstrating different strengths and weaknesses. Einstein excelled at creative visualization skills, but not at language. A company president may have excellent executive skills, but poor social ones.

Sometimes, how well or poorly people perform on a test of some specific cognitive function may have a lot to do with ingrained habits of thought and behavior.

These habits can be hard to tease apart from intelligence, but are nevertheless both changeable and learnable. For example, there is a standard psychological test — used to test for dementia, among other things — in which the subject is asked to name as many fruits, vegetables, or animals as possible in a minute. The more they can name, the higher the score. Many people who do well on this automatically use a strategy of working through the alphabet, using those letters to prompt recollection of words of the right category — for example, *ant, alligator, aardvark, baboon, bird, bear, cheetah, dodo, deer, elephant, eel, flatfish, fly, giraffe, hippo, horse....* (Of course, it is important to move on to the next letter quickly if nothing comes to mind right away.) Other people may work within a more specific, easily visualized subcategory, such as insects *(ant, bluebottle, chigger, deer tick, earwig...).* Any of a number of strategies, perhaps unconsciously applied, can help to increase the number of words generated by "cuing" retrieval of words from the brain's mental lexicon to prevent getting stuck or blanking out.

People who use mnemonic (memory-related) tricks often *seem* to have a better memory even though the trick does not change the way their brain stores data. For example, the salesman's trick of immediately repeating, several times in conversation, the name of a person he has just met helps to consolidate the name in his memory. (For another name-memorizing trick, see the box on page 54.) Other memory aids are, similarly, "crutches" that help along a memory that is less than perfect — always putting keys in the same place, or making a written list of the things to do that day.

Such mnemonic tricks that improve everyday performance do not, as a rule, improve the brain's capacity to store and recall data. On the other hand, if the tricks become automatic and habitual, those people do have a good memory, for certain items at least, and in a *practical* sense that can affect their daily life for the better.

Is there any way that memorization and problem-solving techniques can actually protect or promote the brain's health and agility? For simple tricks like always putting keys in the same place, the answer is probably no. For more cognitively complex skills, and to develop better problem-solving strategies, the answer may well be yes. The very process of figuring out new and effective problem-solving techniques when needed is, itself, rigorous exercise of mental skills and helps keep the brain functional and fit. The next two chapters show how engaging tasks, games, and puzzles can be a crucial part of an "enriched environment" program that may actually help the brain grow new brain connections and protect the ones it already has.

In brief, cognitive skills that are based in the frontal lobes (working memory, executive skills, elaborative encoding) tend to get weaker with age. But this decline is not inevitable: If those skills are used in self-challenging ways in everyday life into old age, they can stay as sharp as they were when young.

Retaining mental flexibility
Along with the executive skills described above, older people tend to have a harder time with mental flexibility.[38] This skill is needed to switch problem-solving strategies in mid-stream as the problem itself evolves or

changes. For example, a traffic hold-up on a route from home to a favorite restaurant may make it sensible to change to another route. Many traditional tests of intelligence and cognitive fitness are more rigid than this. In fact, inventiveness, creativity, and mental flexibility rarely contribute to a higher score in old-style intelligence tests.

One exception to this rule is the test described above in which you have to name as many animals as you can in a minute. This test is open-ended and benefits from mental flexibility. Another is called the Wisconsin Card Sorting Test. This test, widely used for the last 50 years, is intended to detect damage to the frontal lobes caused by stroke or injury. The test also reveals the age-related decline in mental flexibility that is also likely to happen as the frontal lobes become less efficient.[39] The Wisconsin Card Sorting Test requires the person taking the test to figure out, on the basis of feedback from the tester, what the relevant sorting criterion is. The cards can be sorted by color, shape, or number. The examiner places four key cards side by side on the table. The test-taker is then asked to place each of the remaining 128 cards on the table in front of one of the key cards, wherever he or she thinks it should go, with the examiner commenting in each case whether the card is placed correctly or not. Once the

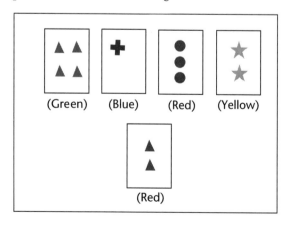

(Green) (Blue) (Red) (Yellow)

(Red)

test-taker has had a chance to figure out the rule (say, "all cards of the same color go together"), the examiner switches the grouping criterion without warning (to, say, "all cards of the same number go together"). Patients with frontal lobe damage can sometimes figure out the initial sorting criterion, but they cannot switch to a new rule when they need to. Instead, they continue to provide the kind of answer the examiner originally called correct, even though such answers are now consistently called wrong. This sort of repeated attempt at the same solution, over and over, despite the need to change strategy, is called *perseveration*. Perseveration problems tend to get worse in old age.

Of course, you can readily see how a mechanized, habitual approach to problem-solving may not be all bad. After all, psychologists are quite proud of pigeons if they can learn to peck at a button of a given color every time they want food. And if a certain solution works every time, one might say that it would be a sign of stupidity to question that solution every time the same problem re-presents itself. But a complex world needs flexibility, and humans need to be far more capable of switching rules flexibly than pigeons. The perseveration that we see in older people when taking the Wisconsin Card Sorting Test, then, is revealing a loss of mental flexibility that may benefit from some of the training methods we will discuss in the next two chapters.

Someone who tries to look at familiar problems in a new light is more likely to come up with a new, and possibly better, solution. For many years, psychologists have used what are sometimes called "*Einstellung* problems" to gauge a person's mental flexibility along these lines (see pages 62 to 65).[40] Einstellung is roughly translatable as habitual orientation or approach — the tendency to apply a certain familiar solution even though the requirements of the problem may change. There does not seem to be a good correlation between Einstellung effects and IQ. In other words, many people of above-average IQ may be only average in creativity and mental flexibility. Traditional IQ tests often fail to pick out those individuals who may have highly original and imaginative approaches to problem-solving. Einstellung tests may therefore be used to pick out those with the most creative approach to real-world problem-solving and planning.

(Continued on page 66)

Frontal-Lobe Flexibility Builder
A perspective-switching game to help your creative thinking skills:

How many grooves are on one side of a 33 rpm phonograph record?

Creative Thinking Quiz
These brain teasers help to give your creative thinking skills a jump-start by challenging you to think about solutions on multiple levels. Are the following statements true or false?

This statement is false.

Their are four errers in this sentance.

(See page 67 for the solutions)

The Jar Game

In this game, you will get three jars of different sizes, and you will have to use those jars to get a certain quantity of water. For a simple example with just two jars, let us say you have a 29-oz. and a 3-oz. jar, and you need to end up with 20 ounces of water:

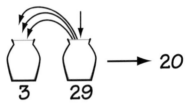

All you have to do is fill the 29-oz. jar, fill the 3-oz. jar three times from the 29-oz. one, and you will end up with 20 ounces:

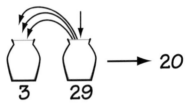

A slightly harder example with three jars goes like this: Say you have a 21-oz., a 127-oz., and a 3-oz. jar, and you have to get 100 ounces of water:

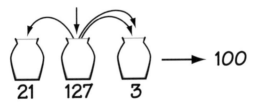

You can solve the problem like this: First, fill the 127-oz. jar, then fill the 21-oz. jar from that, and the 3-oz. jar twice:

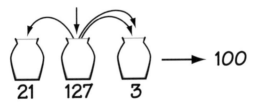

Get the idea? Here are seven problems to solve:
(See page 64 for the solutions)

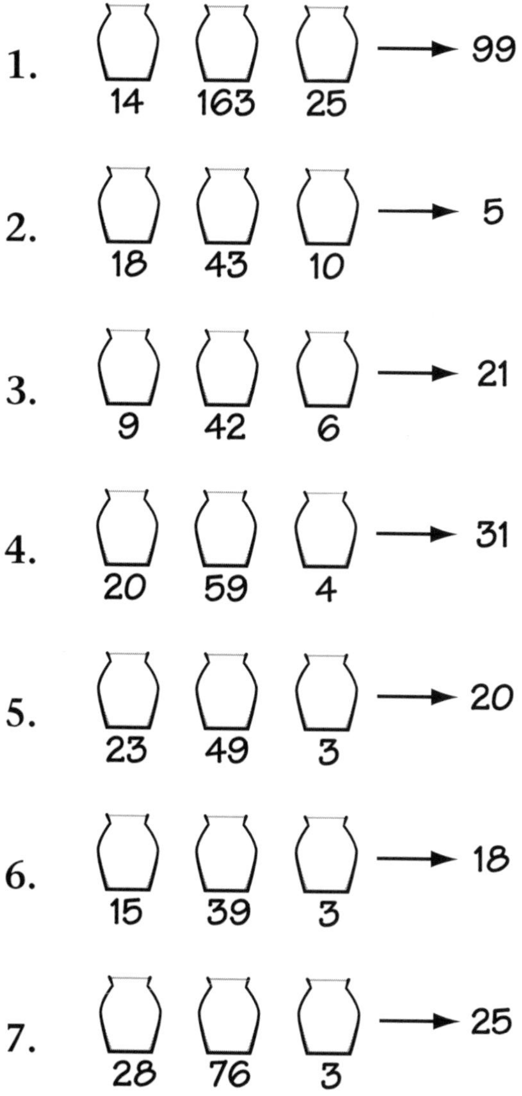

1. 14 163 25 → 99

2. 18 43 10 → 5

3. 9 42 6 → 21

4. 20 59 4 → 31

5. 23 49 3 → 20

6. 15 39 3 → 18

7. 28 76 3 → 25

These are the simplest solutions:
(Solutions for page 63)

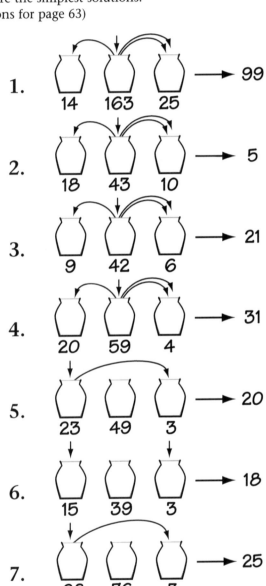

1. 14 163 25 → 99

2. 18 43 10 → 5

3. 9 42 6 → 21

4. 20 59 4 → 31

5. 23 49 3 → 20

6. 15 39 3 → 18

7. 28 76 3 → 25

Of course, problems 5 and 6 also have more complicated solutions involving more moves, on the pattern of 1-4:

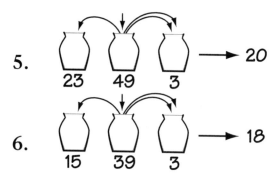

If you persisted in applying the same sort of multi-step solution to these problems as you did to problems 1-4, you were experiencing an *Einstellung* effect: The tendency to apply a certain familiar solution even though the requirements of the problem have changed. For problems 5 and 6, this just results in a more cumbersome solution when a simpler one would have worked. If you still tried applying the familiar solution pattern to problem 7, you would have been stumped, since that old pattern does not work at all for this one.

The kind of mental flexibility required to avoid an Einstellung effect is frontal-lobe-dependent. Older people tend to suffer more from *Einstellung* effects than younger people, just as they tend to have a harder time with many frontal-lobe-dependent skills, such as working memory and executive skills. But these skills can be improved, and maintained, with practice.

(Continued from page 61)

Again, this kind of mental flexibility is not simply something a person is born with, it can be cultivated with practice. Flexible thinking differs from the sorts of abilities that let you score well on intelligence tests. Many creative abilities, and many intellectual abilities that correlate with success in real-world tasks, are simply outside the scope of traditional IQ tests.[41,42] An important group of such abilities is what has been referred to as *divergent* intelligence, distinct from the *convergent* thinking measured by most intelligence tests. A prime example of convergent thinking is the kind involved in deductive logic, as in the famous syllogism: *All men are mortal; Socrates is a man; therefore, Socrates is mortal.* With convergent-thinking problems, there is always — or is supposed to be — a unique solution that the interlocking facts of the available information reveals.

Tasks that require divergent thinking, on the other hand, test imaginative originality, fluency and flexibility of thought, rather than the ability to come up with the right answer. If asked to name as many uses as you can think of for a hammer, the potential list is endless. A good response could be scored in terms of quantity — how many uses can be described in a minute — or quality — how unusual or imaginative the uses are. ("Drive a nail into wood" is obvious; "crack walnuts" is a little less so; and "lean it against an unlockable door to sound an alarm if someone walks into the room at night" would be the least obvious of all.) Divergent

(See page 61)

Frontal-Lobe Flexibility Builder Solution
Only one (one continuous spiral groove).

Creative Thinking Quiz Solution
You cannot really call either statement true or false without encountering a contradiction. For the first one, if you say the statement is true, then the problem is that the statement itself claims to be *false*. If, on the other hand, you say the statement is false, the problem is that the statement itself makes that same claim. For the second one, the three (not four) spelling errors might lead you to believe that the statement is false. In that case, though, the very claim to contain four (not three) errors is also an error, which might make you think the statement is true. But in *that* case, the claim to contain four errors is false. The point with these brain teasers is not to get the right answer, but to run through the logical entailments so that you see the paradoxes. Both run you around in circles, but get your brain going.

ability depends on frontal lobe regions that also support planning and reasoning about possible future events. If these regions are damaged, creative divergent-thinking ability may be impaired but IQ remains perfectly intact.[43]

Can we protect against the effects of aging on memory?

The kinds of memory loss that begin afflicting people as they approach old age can be traced to changes in their brains. In some ways, the course of a person's brain development has a mirror-like quality. The frontal-lobe skills, such as executive and task management skills, elaborative encoding and divergent thinking, are some of the hardest and latest to acquire early in life; they are also some of the easiest to lose later in life. The good news is that functions that change easily, as a result of neglect, for example, can be made to change for the better as well. The most malleable are also the most improvable with practice. The best way to be an expert at organizing information and using it to advantage is to work at it, consistently and often.

The most effective re-training is to tackle real-world puzzles rather than shrink away for fear of failure— stop to plan ahead, for example,to to avoid being literally painted into a corner. Regularly working puzzles purely for entertainment is just as effective because the brain does not perform better if a task is unpleasant. Conditioning of any kind takes more practice and effort at 70 than 30. But, somehow, the rewards are sweeter, especially confidence in managing the challenges of life rather than being managed by them, and satisfaction of meeting crucial problems as they arise.

FOOTNOTES FOR SECTION II

[1] M.A. Luszcz and J. Bryan (1999). Toward understanding age-related memory loss in late adulthood. Gerontology 45:2-9.

[2] M. Sliwinski and H. Buschke (1997). Processing speed and memory in aging and dementia. Journal of Gerontology: Psychological Sciences 52B/6:P308-18.

[3] T.A. Salthouse (1996). The processing-speed theory of adult age differences in cognition. Psychological Review 10:403-28.

[4] J. Myerson et al. (1992) General slowing in semantic priming and word recognition. Psychology and Aging 7:257-70.

[5] A.P. Shimamura et al. (1995). Memory and cognitive abilities in university professors: evidence for successful aging. Psychological Science 6/5:271-7.

[6] D.C. Park et al. (1996). Mediators of long-term memory performance across the life span. Psychology and Aging 11:621-37.

[7] T.A. Salthouse (1996). General and specific speed mediation of adult age differences in memory. Journals of Gerontology, Series B, Psychological Sciences and Social Sciences 51B:P30-42.

[8] J. Bryan and M.A. Luszcz (1996). Speed of information processing as a mediator between age and free-recall performance. Psychology and Aging 18/3:383-93.

[9] D. Bartsch et al. (1995). Aplysia CREB2 represses long-term facilitation. Cell 83:979-92.

[10] T.J. Grabowski, H. Damasio, and A.R. Damasio (1998). Premotor and prefrontal correlates of category-related lexical retrieval. Neuroimage 7/3:232-43.

[11] D.D. Woodruff-Pak (1997). The Neuropsychology of Aging. Oxford: Blackwell.

[12] R.L. West (1996). An application of prefrontal cortex function theory to cognitive aging. Psychological Bulletin 120:272-92.

[13] D.L. Schacter (1996).

[14] E.F. Loftus and J.E. Pickrell (1995). The formation of false memories. Psychiatric Annals 25:720-5.

[15] A. Baddeley (1986). Working Memory Oxford: Clarendon Press.

[16] M.D. Lezak (1995). Neuropsychological Assessment, 3rd ed. New York: Oxford University Press.

[17] A.P. Shimamura (1995). Memory and frontal lobe function. In M.S. Gazzaniga (ed.), The Cognitive Neurosciences. Cambridge MA: MIT Press, 803-13.

[18] M. Moscovitch and G. Winocar (1992). The neuropsychology of memory and aging.

[19] A. Bechara et al. (1996). Failure to respond autonomically to anticipated future outcomes following damage to prefrontal cortex. Cerebral Cortex 6:215-25.

[20] M.A. Luszcz and J. Bryan (1999).

[21] A.J. Parkin and B.M. Walter (1992). Recollective experience, normal aging, and frontal dysfunction. Psychology and Aging 2:290-8.

22 S. Daigneault and C.M.J. Braun (1993). Working memory and the self-ordered pointing task: further evidence of early prefrontal decline in normal aging. Journal of Clinical and Experimental Neuropsychology 15:881-95.

23 M.S. Albert and M.B. Moss (1996). Neuropsychology of aging: findings in humans and monkeys. In E. Schneider and J.W. Rowe (eds.), The Handbook of the Biology of Aging, 4th ed.. San Diego: Academic Press.

24 D. Schretlen et al. (2000). Evaluating the contributions of processing speed, executive ability, and frontal lobe volume to normal age-related differences in fluid intelligence. Journal of the International Neuropsychological Society 6/1:52-61.

25 M. Hartman and L. Hasher (1991). Aging and suppression: memory for previously relevant information. Psychology and Aging 6:587-94.

26 L. Hasher et al. (1991). Age and inhibition. Journal of Experimental Psychology: Learning, Memory, and Cognition 17:163-9.

27 D.L. Schacter (1996).

28 E.F. Loftus and J.E. Pickrell (1995).

29 A.P. Shimamura et al. (1995).

30 N.D. Volkow et al. (2000). Association between age-related decline in brain dopamine activity and impairment in frontal and cingulate metabolism. American Journal of Psychiatry 157/1: 75-80.

31 G. Garraux et al. (1999). Comparison of impaired subcortico-frontal metabolic networks in normal aging, subcortico-frontal dementia, and cortical frontal dementia. Neuroimage 10/2:149-62.

32 A.J. Parkin and B.M. Walter (1992).

33 F.I.M. Craik et al. (1995). Memory changes in normal aging. In A.D. Baddeley, B.A. Wilson, and F. N. Watt (eds.), Handbook of Memory Disorders. New York: Wiley.

34 D.L. Schacter (1996).

35 Grady et al. (1995). Age-related reductions in human recognition memory due to impaired encoding. Science 269:218-21.

[36] R. Cabeza et al. (1997). Age-related differences in effective neural connectivity during encoding and recall. Neuroreport 8:3479-83.

[37] Grady et al. (1995).

[38] S. Belleville et al. (1996). Examination of the working memory components in normal aging and in dementia of the Alzheimer's type. Neuropsychologia 34:195-207.

[39] M.D. Lezak (1995).

[40] A.S. Luchins (1942). Mechanization in problem solving: the effect of Einstellung. Psychological monographs 54/6.

[41] R.J. Sternberg (1985). Beyond IQ: A triarchic theory of human intelligence. Cambridge: Cambridge University Press.

[42] H. Gardner (1999). Intelligence Reframed: Multiple intelligences for the 21st Century. New York: Basic Books.

[43] B. Milner and M. Petrides (1984). Behavioural effects of frontal-lobe lesions in man. Trends in Neurosciences November 1984: 403-7.

COMMON COGNITIVE PROBLEMS THAT ARE NOT ALZHEIMER'S

and what you can do about them

EVALUATING THE SOURCES
OF COGNITIVE PROBLEMS

COMMON SUBSTANCES THAT
MAY HARM THE BRAIN

IF YOU DO HAVE ALZHEIMER'S

COMMON COGNITIVE PROBLEMS THAT ARE NOT ALZHEIMER'S

EVALUATING THE SOURCES OF COGNITIVE PROBLEMS

When lapses in memory, especially of recent events, begin to show up consistently and seem to increase in frequency, do not hesitate to make an appointment for a cognitive evaluation by a physician. It is important to begin a process of evaluation when such memory lapses first appear because many signs of apparent cognitive decline are not due to Alzheimer's (AD) at all, and are readily treated once the real underlying cause is diagnosed.

If the signs of cognitive decline are professionally diagnosed as AD, even though no absolute cure is yet known, there are treatments that can slow the progression of the disease. Chapter four describes how lifestyle changes can also help to combat dementia even after it is started. Specific treatments will be presented later.

Is it dementia? Or could it be depression?

The relationship between depression and dementia, including AD, is complex. Depression is common in AD patients. A recent brain-scan study showed decreased activity in the frontal lobes of depressed AD patients.[1] There are two ways of looking at these results. One explanation is that depression could well be a symptom of the cluster of brain changes brought about by the disease. It may also in some cases be an emotional response to a conscious fear of cognitive decline. Many researchers suspect that depression may be a *risk factor* for the gradual onset of dementia. Some studies even appear to show that people with a history of depression are at greater risk for AD.[2,3]

On the other hand, the symptoms of depression have a lot in common with the early symptoms of AD. Some of the most common symptoms of depression also occur in AD. Inattentiveness, disorientation, forgetfulness, and mental lethargy are frequently reported in both conditions. To compound the confusion between the symptoms, all of them can be especially pronounced in depressed older people. In fact, they resemble the cognitive impairments of AD so closely that the two can be very difficult to tell apart, even for a trained medical professional (see pages 76 to 78).

Unlike true AD symptoms, the dementia-like symptoms of depression are relatively treatable and reversible. Depression often follows withdrawal from social, mental, and physical stimulation, especially in older people. This kind of withdraw-
al, which is very likely to occur when one retires from work, can be described as retirement syndrome. Unfortunately, when they retire, many people lose their motivation to tax their brains. For one thing they reduce the variety of their social contacts and, as well,

(Continued on page 79)

Delayed Recall

Several versions of delayed word recall test have been used to help distinguish people with early Alzheimer's from those who are just depressed.

In this version, there are two shopping lists (Monday and Friday). What you are going to try to do is memorize the items on each list, first Monday and then Friday.

It helps to have an "examiner" for this. If you do not, just follow the instructions for the examiner and cover up the list as you write down your answers.

Monday	*Tuesday*
oranges	bananas
wrench	corkscrew
rosemary	peppercorns
pineapple	apples
thumbtacks	can opener
socks	oysters
salt	basil
swimsuit	sardines
hammer	mixing bowl
grapes	lemons
paprika	bay leaf
sandals	tuna
plums	apricots
oregano	cinnamon
t-shirt	measuring cup
shovel	flounder

Examiner:

1) Read these instructions out loud to the person taking the test:

   "I am going to read you a shopping list. Pay attention, because as soon as I'm done reading the list I want you to repeat back to me as many of the items as you can remember, in any order you like."

2) Then, read the Monday list out loud, slowly and clearly, about one word per second.

3) As soon as you are done reading the list, ask the test-taker to recite out loud as many items from the list as possible, writing down each item as the test-taker names it. Once the test-taker cannot recall any more items, read Monday's list out loud once more, and ask him or her once again to recite as many as possible, including ones already recited the first time. Repeat this procedure three more times, for a total of five run-throughs.

4) Next, read the following instructions:

   "I'm now going to read you a different list. Pay attention clearly so you remember as many of the items as possible."

5) Then, read Friday's list out loud, slowly and clearly. Once you are done, ask the test-taker to recall as many items from the list as possible, but this time do it only once. Then, ask the test-taker once again to recall as many items from Monday's list as possible, writing down the answers as they are recited.

6) Finally, after a delay of 30 minutes, ask the test-taker once again to recite as many items as possible from the first (Monday's) list.

(Continued on page 78)

(Continued from page 77)

Scoring norms for people under 65 years old:
After the first run-through of the list:
    5 items or under remembered from the first list: Needs work
    6-8 words: Good
    9-10 words: Excellent
    11+ : Extraordinary

After the fifth run-through:
    10 or under: Needs work
    11-12: Good
    13-14: Excellent
    15-16: Extraordinary

These norms fall off with age. Women also perform better than men, on average. This might be because women seem to be better at organizing the list using categories, for example by putting all the fruit together. This makes it easier for them to remember the list. Psychologists call this a "semantic clustering" strategy. However, the use of a semantic clustering strategy also tends to fall off with age. Older people tend to make more errors of falsely supplying a word that was not on the list. These intrusion errors include interference errors, such as reciting some of the first list's items in recall of the second list (proactive interference), or the second list's items in the recall of the first list (retroactive interference). You may want to refer back to the discussion of these terms in more detail in Chapter 2.

Scoring norms for people with Alzheimer's:
People with early-stage Alzheimer's tend to recall hardly any items on the first trial, and only about five to six items on the fifth trial. Alzheimer's patients also tend to make far more intrusion errors (over one third of their responses tend to be words that did not appear on the actual list) than healthy people of the same age. Also, they tend to forget most of the items on the list in the delayed recall stage (after 30 minutes), unlike healthy people of the same age, who recall most of them.

(Continued from page 75)

any urgent need to analyze and solve thorny problems as they were forced to regularly in the normal course of a working day. Unless replaced with the cognitive challenges of other active interests and social interactions, the cost of a relaxed retirement may be the beginning of noticeable cognitive impairment. Depression may, therefore, be caused by the effect an isolated, routine lifestyle exerts on the chemical messenger systems within the brain. There have been rapid advances in the development of drugs that can help to balance the messenger systems involved in depression, so it is important to diagnose and treat it.

Symptoms caused by the side-effects of medication
As bodies age, they function less well. Old injuries or other conditions start acting up. Older people start taking more medications to relieve new aches and inconveniences. Most medications cause side effects some of which produce the same medical and emotional symptoms caused by physical deterioration of brain circuits. Older bodies become less efficient at getting rid of the medications after they have had their beneficial effects. Older people tend to take more medications than younger people, especially sleeping pills and drugs for heart disease, which often cause dementia-like symptoms, especially if several of them are taken together. If mental decline is due to medication alternatives might be considered.

Sleeping pills, for example, are common culprits in medication-induced mental confusion. Sleeping pill abuse is often a result of depression, because poor sleep and depression often go hand in hand in the elderly.

Lifestyle causes of depression, such as social, mental, and physical inactivity, can cause sleep problems as well. Antidepressant medications can cause forgetfulness, disorientation, and inattentiveness in some people. A program of increasing social, mental, and physical stimulation, known as *environmental enrichment,* may often be effective in combatting both depression and the dementia-like symptoms caused by medication use.

In extreme cases, alcoholism may lead to Wernicke-Korsakoff syndrome, an irreversible disorder with symptoms of amnesia and confusion. More commonly, excessive alcohol consumption for a decade or more can cause an AD-like dementia marked by memory, orientation, and attention impairments. This kind of alcohol-induced dementia is at least partly reversible.

Small strokes can cause dementia
Tiny strokes, sometimes called "mini-strokes," are caused by small interruptions in the supply of blood to groups of brain cells, producing a small area of dead brain tissue, known as an *infarct.* A sufficient accumulation of tiny strokes can cause what is called *multi-infarct dementia. Transient ischemic attacks* (TIAs) are different from mini-strokes. In fact, signs of their presence cannot even be seen in a brain scan. They do not cause dementia but they are signs that the brain is at risk for serious strokes that could. While multi-infarct dementia is not as easily treated as dementia caused by depression, medication or alcohol, reducing high blood pressure can often help avoid future mini-strokes.

COMMON SUBSTANCES THAT MAY HARM THE BRAIN

Whether you have dementia or not: How to help your brain to stay healthy

Over the last fifty years the percentage and gross number of people living into their eighties and beyond has increased enormously. The main reason that symptoms of dementia have become more and more common is that there are more people around whose bodies are living longer so the declining health of their brains shows up dramatically.

Why do some functions decline as we age? There are many answers to this question. First, on the level of evolution and natural selection, it is likely that mammals are not programmed to stay fit beyond their prime reproductive and child-rearing years. Specific, wholly natural, biological mechanisms appear to cause the brain to self-destruct. In fact, some parts of the brain appear to let themselves be destroyed without fighting back. Continuing research into specific mechanisms of brain destruction may reveal practical ways to manipulate or augment the brain's own self-repair and self-maintenance systems. The long-term benefit of this research, obviously, could

Vitamin E: Natural protection for your brain cells

contribute to our understanding of how to remain cognitively fit throughout life.

Programmed cell death: **Brain cell suicide**

The mechanisms causing biological self-destruction of brain structures have attracted a lot of scientific and media attention recently. In some kinds of brain disease or injury, brain cells die because they produce self-destructive chemicals, or because they simply fail to take the necessary steps to keep themselves alive. In effect, they commit suicide. Some experiments have shown that the body gradually withdraws supportive, nutritive brain proteins called *growth factors* that normally sustain brain cells. As a result, the brain cells produce "killer proteins" that cause their own death.[4,5,6] Brain-cell suicide can be delayed by increasing the supply of natural growth factors. Growth factor production can be increased by mental and physical exercise, surgical implants, and in some other ways which are discussed in the next chapter.

Free Radicals: Destructive brain-toxic chemicals

Highly reactive hydrogen, oxygen, and iron molecules with extra electrons, called "free radicals", can be produced within the brain after brain injury. They also occur in a number of brain-based and brain-damaging disorders, such as chronic alcoholism, epilepsy, and AD. They kill brain cells by punching holes in the cell's protective membrane, releasing survival-essential substances and letting in toxins. Free radicals can be produced outside the brain by a wide variety of diseases and in response to lifestyle stressors. Indeed, aging itself is believed to increase free radical production and lead to heightened oxidative brain-tissue damage.

Vitamin E: Natural protection for your brain cells
One of the best-known forms of protection against free radicals are called *antioxidants,* also known as *free radical scavengers.* Vitamins C and E are both antioxidants. A variety of animal experiments over the past ten years has shown that vitamin E is effective in combatting brain damage. In one experiment, rats given vitamin E injections after frontal lobe removal performed just as well on frontal-lobe-based intelligence tests as rats with undamaged frontal lobes.[7] Other experiments have used rats whose carotid artery was blocked, which normally causes serious neuron loss and brain damage because it cuts off the supply of oxygen and fuel to the brain. These rats suffered little brain-cell loss if they were given vitamin E injections.[8]

Vitamin E might therefore guard against brain-cell damage both by scavenging free radicals and by protecting the membranes that surround brain cells, thus combatting a broad range of changes in the brain that occur in AD. For example, the defining symptoms of AD is the presence of *plaques* in the substance outside brain cells. These plaques consist mainly of a protein called *beta-amyloid,* which in an Alzheimer's diseased brain is cleaved off of a beneficial protein called *APP.* It has always intrigued researchers that, while amyloid plaques appear to be a consistent symptom of AD, some people have the plaques without any *behavioral* symptoms of the disease — in other words, they retain good memory and general cognitive skills. Vitamin E may be capable of protecting cells from beta-amyloid and amyloid plaques by fighting free radicals produced by the rogue protein.

Although the experiments with rats mentioned above relied on injections or implanted pumps to get vitamin E into the brain — a procedure one obviously cannot try at home — there are simpler ways of getting the brain-protecting benefit of this antioxidant. Other experiments have shown that dietary supplements can increase brain levels of vitamin E by 50 to 100%.[9,10,11] The Alzheimer's Disease Cooperative Study (a consortium of Alzheimer's research centers, sponsored by the National Institute on Aging) has planned a clinical trial to determine whether dietary supplements of vitamin E can forestall the development of AD in older people with mild cognitive impairment.[12] Meanwhile, many experts recommend vitamin E supplements for older people with memory complaints. Such supplements could provide an inexpensive, independently beneficial nutrient that the available evidence indicates may well help to keep the brain healthy.

Ginkgo Biloba and cholinesterase inhibitors

Extracts from the *ginkgo biloba* tree, which have been part of the Chinese pharmacopoeia for millennia, have been the subjects of trials in Europe and North America which produced claims of beneficial effects on memory and alertness. Neuroscientific research has not yet found clear proof establishing that either ginkgo or cholinesterase inhibitors are capable of improving cognitive performance in patients even suffering from mild to moderate dementia of the Alzheimer's type.

The exact mechanism by which ginkgo might have any benefit is still a subject of investigation. Research has not verified claims of anti-clotting and antioxidant properties, or that it boosts the supply of blood to the brain. Like vitamin E, it is low-risk and non-invasive, so it is sometimes recommended for its effectiveness as a placebo to those with mild cognitive impairment or memory complaints.

The role of melatonin

Melatonin, a hormone secreted by the pineal gland, has a popular reputation for antioxidant benefits to the brain. The level of melatonin in the bloodstream increases at night time normally, but, as the body ages the night time level decreases significantly. Melatonin helps to regulate the brain's circadian "clock," and its drop in production with age is one reason elderly people normally sleep fewer hours. There is no scientific evidence that it can act as an antioxidant except in doses so large no one would consider it. Melatonin supplements are currently being tested on patients suffering from AD by the Alzheimer's Disease Cooperative Study, in an attempt to determine their effectiveness in combatting sleep problems common in Alzheimer's.[13]

Melatonin's true value is that it may also be beneficial to older people without dementia, both for its possible neuron-protecting effects and its ability to promote good sleep.

Estrogen

A number of prescription drugs have possible antioxidant properties as well. Researchers have shown that women who have been taking supplements of the hormone *estrogen* show a reduced risk for Alzheimer's and other dementias. Estrogen replacement therapy was intended to combat post-menopausal health risks such as osteoporosis and heart disease but recent information suggests it does not protect the heart. Very recent research has suggested that estrogen levels, while lower among all women after menopause than earlier in life, are particularly low in women with AD.[14] In other words, estrogen seems to help protect against dementia.

A large body of research since the mid-nineties on the connection between estrogen and Alzheimer's has pointed to several mechanisms by which this hormone may forestall dementia.[15] It promotes the growth of dendrites — that is, helps brain cells to stay high-functioning by replacing lost connections between them. Estrogen also helps maintain the brain's *cholinergic system* in areas typically harmed by AD. The cholinergic system is the system that releases the neurotransmitter acetylcholine, crucial for proper attention and memory functions. Estrogen also appears, like ginkgo, melatonin, and vitamin E, to have antioxidant properties, and so to have the ability to protect brain cells from damage by free radical substances. Fortunately, recent research indicates that older women don't need to have been on estrogen replacement therapy for a long time in order to benefit. Older women with only a very brief exposure to estrogen supplements show improvements in cognition as well — including those who have no dementia symptoms.[16]

Another prescription drug claimed to be effective in improving cognition among moderately-impaired Alzheimer's patients is *selegiline,* a medication used with Parkinson's patients that raises the levels of a variety of neurotransmitters within the brain. As with estrogen, one of the ways selegiline is said to work is by virtue of its antioxidant properties. Though it is claimed to raise levels of neurotransmitters that are generally low in Alzheimer's patients there is no scientific evidence of its effectiveness for AD.[17]

Stress hormones: deadly to brain cells
Cortisol is a harmful, brain-toxic substance that is produced naturally by the body. It is one of a class of hormones released by the adrenal glands when the body is under stress. Cortisol reduces the blood-glucose energy supply to the brain, causing mental confusion and difficulties with short-term memory. It also interferes with the brain's neurotransmitters, crucial for proper communication from one brain cell to another. Eventually, high levels of cortisol resulting from chronic stress can kill brain cells by stimulating the production of free radicals. Chronically high levels of cortisol are bad under any circumstances, and they may play a role in causing dementia. Research has shown that high levels of cortisol are present in patients with AD.

One way the body can combat this harmful hormone is

by reducing exposure to stress, and by learning to control response to stress. Relaxation techniques such as yoga, meditation, and biofeedback appear to help some people, as do enjoyable mental and social stimulation and physical exercise. Regular exercise also helps counteract brain degeneration because physically fit people tend to have a milder stress response which, in turn, lowers cortisol levels. Aerobic exercise also boosts the supply of blood to the brain, which promotes mental clarity, and helps keep the cardiovascular system in good shape. Neurons draw on more energy when they are forced to become active. Increasing blood flow to the brain supplies the fuel neurons need on an ongoing basis.

All the brain-harming substances just discussed are ones that everyone should watch out for, whether AD is a real or imagined threat to their lives. For those who now are struggling against AD, or for the people who are caring for them, take heart. In the last year, a great deal of serious, well-funded research into the causes and possible cures for AD in laboratory animals is beginning to translate into a few promising pharmaceutical products currently undergoing trials for practical application to the human condition. That is urgent work for the 4 million current sufferers. That number will quadruple to epidemic proportions when the baby boomers enter old age.

IF YOU DO HAVE ALZHEIMER'S DISEASE

Current and future medications for combatting AD

One of the earliest theories about the cause of AD is that the disease stems from problems with the brain system that produces and responds to the chemical *acetylcholine,* a vital "memory" neurotransmitter.[18] This theory is based partly on the fact that the cognitive skills of attention and memory that acetylcholine supports are some of the first skills that deteriorate in AD. More decisively, biopsies of the brains of AD patients show that it is mainly the neurons of the *cholinergic* system (the network of brain cells producing and responding to acetylcholine) that are harmed or destroyed early in the disease's progression. Also, levels of acetylcholine are lowest in AD patients with the most severe cognitive problems.

The notion that AD could be caused by a shortage of acetylcholine has led to the development of drugs that raise its levels within the brain. They do this by blocking the enzyme that breaks down acetylcholine after it has been released into the synapse (the communication junction between brain cells). This should, in theory, raise acetylcholine levels and help ensure the survival of neurons in the cholinergic system.

Drugs that inhibit the enzyme that breaks down acetyl-choline have already been developed and are available by prescription. Donepezil, marketed under the brand name *Aricept*, is already available by prescription though it does not effectively slow down the course of developing dementia. Some other drugs, including rivastigmine (brand name *Exelon*) and metrifonate are undergoing or have undergone trials and will be available soon in the United States.[19] Like antidepressants, some of these drugs also raise levels of the serotonin neurotransmitter, which tends to improve mood.

There is no clear scientific evidence that drugs that work on the cholinergic system are to be effective in slowing the progression of AD, and they are certainly not cures. As placebo or not, their clinical affect is said to work in the early stages before the symptoms become too severe. If so, early detection would help to maximize their effectiveness.

What the genetic research tells us
Along with increasingly sophisticated brain-imaging technology, the mapping of the human genome has fueled an explosion of knowledge about the brain. The more accurately geneticists can identify exactly which genes do what, the better neuroscientists can tease out the causes of physical and mental illnesses such as Parkinson's, depression, AD, and so on — on a genetic level.

In the case of AD, several genetic risk factors have been identified. Humans have about 80,000 genes, which contain the recipes used to manufacture all the many types of proteins which build and maintain our bodies. The genes are contained in structures called chromosomes. A full set of chromosomes is present in each cell in the body. A defective gene on chromosome 21, which builds a protein known as APP, has been argued to cause some forms of AD. People with this mutant gene are very likely to develop the amyloid deposits characteristic of brains that show AD-type degeneration.

Another gene found to be involved in AD is called (appropriately enough) *presenilin*. A mutated form of this gene also results in increased production of the substance that forms amyloid plaques. In a recent experiment on mice that were genetically defective so that they would develop amyloid deposits, scientists claimed success in immunizing the mice against overproduction of the harmful amyloid substance, thus preventing the production of amyloid deposits.[20] This raises the very real prospect of the development of a human vaccine against AD. It is important to keep in mind, however, that both the APP and the presenilin genes, which have been linked to early-onset AD, account for only a small number of AD cases. Early-onset AD (which strikes before age 65, and has a clear genetic basis) is uncommon. In most cases, signs of AD appear only after age 65, with the risk rising with increased age. The more common late-onset AD has a much weaker genetic basis than early-onset AD.

One gene that does appear to play a role in some instances of late-onset AD produces a protein called *apolipoprotein E* (ApoE), believed by some researchers to play a critical role in maintaining the supply of vital nutrients to brain cells. The ApoE protein has three variants, each of which produces a slightly different version of the protein.

Every person inherits a variant of the ApoE gene from each parent, with the result that there are many possible combinations. Research at Duke University has determined that one of the variants, known as e4, confers a high risk for developing AD, especially if it is inherited from both parents.[21] In fact, in this Duke University study, 91% of people who inherited e4 from both parents developed AD.

Again, though, genetics is only part of the story with late-onset AD. For one thing, the risk of developing late-onset AD is only slightly higher if one's parents, brothers, or sisters had, or has, AD. Also, only 3% of the population inherits the e4 variant of the ApoE gene from both parents. More than half the population, in fact, has the desirable e3/e3 combination. And finally, lacking the e4 variant of the gene does not guarantee one will not get AD: The same researchers determined that just 64% of AD patients without a family history of the disease had one or more e4 alleles.

AD has many causes
AD experts agree that AD, like dementia in general, is not a single disease with a single cause. Certain genes may predispose some people to AD, but not everyone, and others may develop AD without that genetic risk. Many lifestyle factors may play a role in turning a genetic AD risk into reality, and destructive habits of thought and behavior can in themselves be sufficient to cause impaired cognition and perhaps even dementia.

So much press is given to AD disease these days that we are all being distracted from some very important facts: There are many possible causes of apparent cognitive decline in adulthood and old age, and many of those causes respond readily to fairly low-tech treatment. Sometimes the treatment is as simple as making sure that you have enough social contact, mental stimulation, and physical exercise to keep your brain healthy. And while we are all waiting for an AD cure, we should not forget that many of the same factors that are bad for our brain at age 30 or 40 may also contribute to developing AD later in life. Finally, as more and more drugs and medications are developed to help reduce the risk of AD or to slow the progression of the disease once it starts, it is essential to keep in mind that those medications work better if they are accompanied by the things that have the power to help maintain a healthy brain in the first place.

FOOTNOTES FOR SECTION III

[1] N. Hirono et al. (1998). Frontal lobe hypometabolism and depression in Alzheimer's disease. Neurology 50/2:380-3.

[2] C.E. Speck et al. (1995). History of depression as a risk factor for Alzheimer's disease. Epidemiology 6/4:366-9.

[3] M.F. Weiner, S.D. Edland, and H. Luszczynska (1994). Prevalence and incidence of major depression in Alzheimer's disease. American Journal of Psychiatry 151/7:1006-9.

4 T.L Deckwerth and E.M. Johnson Jr. (1993). Temporal analysis of events associated with programmed cell death (apoptosis) of sympathetic neurons deprived of nerve growth factor. Journal of Cell Biology 123/5:1207-22.

5 J.M. Frade and Y.A. Barde (1998). Nerve growth factor: two receptors, multiple functions. Bio essays 20/2.

6 K.M. Rich (1992). Neuronal death after trophic factor deprivation. Journal of Neurotrauma 9 (Suppl. 1):S61-9.

7 P.G. Stein, M. Halks-Miller, and S.W. Hoffman (1991). Intracerebral administration of alpha-tocopherol-containing liposomes facilitates behavioral recovery in rats with bilateral lesions of the frontal cortex. Journal of Neurotrauma 8/4:281-92.

8 S. Inci, O.E. Ozcan, and K. Kilinc (1998). Time-level relationship for lipid peroxidation and the protective effect of alpha-tocopherol in experimental mild and severe brain injury. Neurosurgery 43/2:330-5.

9 Michael Grundman (2000). Vitamin E and Alzheimer's disease: the basis for additional clinical trials. American Journal of Clinical Nutrition 71 (Suppl.):630S-6S.

10 M. Meydani, J.B. Macauley, and J.B. Blumberg (1988). Effect of dietary vitamin E and selenium on susceptibility of brain regions to lipid peroxidation. Lipids 23:405-9.

11 A. Monji et al. (1994). Effect of dietary vitamin E on lipofuscin accumulation with age in the rat brain. Brain Research 634:62-8.

12 Michael Grundman (2000). Vitamin E and Alzheimer's disease: the basis for additional clinical trials. American Journal of Clinical Nutrition 71 (Suppl.):630S-6S.

13 W.M.H. Behan et al. (1999). Oxidative stress as a mechanism for quinolinic acid-induced hippocampal damage: protection by melatonin and deprynyl. British Journal of Pharmacology 128:1754-60.

14 J.J. Manly et al. (2000). Endogenous estrogen levels and Alzheimer's disease among postmenopausal women. Neurology 54:833-7.

15 Joan Stephenson (1996). More evidence links NSAID, estrogen use with reduced Alzheimer risk. Journal of the American Medical Association 275/18:1389-90

[16] D.M. Jacobs et al. (1998). Cognitive function in nondemented women who took estrogen after menopause. Neurology 50:368-73.

[17] Mary Sano et al. (1997). A controlled trial of selegiline, alpha-tocopherol, or both as treatment for Alzheimer's disease. The New England Journal of Medicine 336/17:1216-22.

[18] P.T. Francis et al. (1999). The cholinergic hypothesis of Alzheimer's disease: a review of progress. Journal of Neurology, Neurosurgery, and Psychiatry 66/2:137-47.

[19] P.T. Francis et al. (1999). The cholinergic hypothesis of Alzheimer's disease: a review of progress. Journal of Neurology, Neurosurgery, and Psychiatry 66/2:137-47.

[20] Dale Schenk et al. (1999). Immunization with amyloid-beta attenuates Alzheimer-disease-like pathology in the PDAPP mouse. Nature 400:173-7.

[21] A.D. Roses (1994). Apolipoprotein E affects the rate of Alzheimer's disease expression: beta-amyloid burden is a secondary consequence dependent on APOE genotype and duration of disease. Journal of Neuropathology and Experimental Neurology 53/5:429-37

SECTION IV

PREVENTING AND REVERSING COGNITIVE DECLINE WITH AGE

based on current research results

OUTMODED BELIEFS
ABOUT THE BRAIN

NEW FINDINGS

PRACTICAL WAYS TO
APPLY RESULTS

COMMON SUBSTANCES
IN THE BODY THAT MAY
HELP THE BRAIN

Preventing and Reversing Cognitive Decline with Age

Outmoded Beliefs About the Brain

The dogma in brain science has long been that "in the adult brain, nervous pathways are fixed and immutable; everything may die, nothing may be regenerated." This pessimistic view, put forward by Nobel Prize-winning Spanish neuroscientist Ramón y Cajal over 60 years ago, has discouraged interest in developing drugs, treatments, and therapies for brain-damaging injuries and diseases such as stroke and AD, as well as for common age-related cognitive decline.

Another traditional, and incorrect, view of the brain is that any mental ability or function — language, memory, motivation — is housed in a specific part of the brain. This view dates from the 19th century, when practitioners of the pseudoscience of *phrenology* claimed to be able to gauge a person's intelligence and even moral rectitude by "reading" the bumps and contours on the skull; they imagined that the bumps were shaped by the brain beneath. In many ways, this belief in the separation of different skills in different areas of the human brain is still with us, and leads us to overemphasize the degree to which specific brain functions are localized in specific areas. Even in experiments using sophisticated imaging technology, such as PET or fMRI, researchers may simplify complex, widespread patterns of brain activation in their search for *the* brain region underlying a skill such as reading, or a disability such as dyslexia.

In the brain, redundancy is good

Dramatic evidence contradicts the idea that the human brain develops from a strict blueprint that assigns specific functions to specific regions. In a rare brain operation called a *hemispherectomy*, one half of the cortex of the brain is entirely removed in order to correct severe epileptic seizures. It is a remarkable fact that, even when the left hemisphere is removed completely, carrying away with it the dominant language regions of the brain, a young patient under a certain age will recover full language ability within a relatively short period of time. What accounts for this recovery? The right hemisphere does not re-learn language skills from scratch. The explanation is that even though the left hemisphere processes nearly all language skills in most people, regions of the right hemisphere still have some relatively passive language skills that will become fully activated only if the left-brain regions are destroyed.

Even though this kind of redundancy and flexibility is most pronounced in children, it is never completely lost. In brain scan studies of adults whose dominant left hemisphere controls language, regions of the right side of the brain still show some activation during language tasks. This same kind of imaging technology reveals that many brain regions reorganize themselves after an adult suffers a brain injury such as a stroke.

The human brain's ability to share tasks spontaneously when needed does not support the older, modular view that the different mental functions are rigidly localized in specific brain regions. The modular view implies that once a single discrete brain region is lost to disease or injury, the function associated with that region can never be recovered. More encouraging recent advances in brain research are making it increasingly clear that the adult human brain has built-in mechanisms for adjusting to and compensating for brain injury.

In fact, the plasticity of the human brain may account for the survival of our species. The large brain has allowed humans to foresee and plan ahead to invent ways to adapt successfully to changing conditions. Interestingly, the large trove of neurons in the human brain appears *itself* to change its ways to fit the demands of survival.

Recent research has also overturned the traditional view that adult central nervous system cells cannot regenerate. In fact, neurogenesis has now been documented not just in laboratory animals and in isolated cells grown in the laboratory, but in adult human brains.[1,2]

New Findings

How to keep your brain cells healthy: "Use it or lose it" vs. "wear and tear"

It is becoming clear that science now can show specifically how the "use it or lose it" concept applies to the functions of the brain. First though, it is worth reviewing *other* ideas that have been proposed in the past to explain why brains change as they develop and age. Current advice about the importance of maintaining brain-based skills is so sensible and intuitive that it is easy to adopt wholeheartedly. So it may come as a shock to learn that an influential doctrine in the study of the aging brain has been essentially the opposite of the "use it or lose it" idea — namely, the model sometimes referred to as "wear and tear." The "wear and tear" model promoted the idea that what happens as a person gets older is that brain cells, like certain other parts of the body or like the brake pads on a car, gradually get worn down by use. How might that happen?

There is evidence that ordinary by-products of cell metabolism, such as what are called free radicals (see Chapter 3), can damage neurons. (One way they cause damage is by harming the cells' ability to maintain themselves or create new dendrites.) Certain "stress" hormones known as glucocorticoids, naturally produced in the body, have also been shown to interfere with brain function and even kill neurons when their levels are high. Even oxygen can damage brain cells if its level is too high. Perhaps, then, our brains slow down as we age simply as the result of a wearing away of brain cells, or a decreased ability of neurons to respond to new challenges, because the very fact of living exposes our brain cells to toxins. So those cells, sooner or later, wear out or die and force us into senility the way the inevitable erosion of cartilage in a catcher's knee forces him to retire from baseball by the time he reaches his mid-thirties.

What the "wear and tear" model ignores, though, is the fact that brain cells have self-support and regeneration mechanisms that are actually *stimulated* by use. Dutch researcher David Swaab (one of the foremost proponents of the "use it or lose it" approach) has pointed out that the use of neurons may protect them. Stimulating brain cells can also help avoid brain degeneration with age, by boosting genetically triggered repair mechanisms that enable the cells to maintain themselves and grow.[3] Mental effort may also trigger the production of the brain's own natural antioxidants. The "use it or lose it" principle may in fact provide a better explanation for the effect of glucocorticoids than the "wear and tear" model because excess glucocorticoids impede the fuel uptake of cells, thereby interfering with their proper function. Swaab adds that it is not *increased* activity of certain brain regions that correlates with AD, but *decreased* activity.[4] AD brains show a reduction in the products of genetically triggered repair, and the brain areas affected by AD show decreased metabolism. The obvious chicken-and-egg problem has not yet been resolved: Does decreased activity lead to

AD, or is it the other way around? As Swaab reminds us, it is still an open question, and both possibilities need to be investigated.

If the "use it or lose it" concept is truly valid when applied to the brain, then how could it be that, as Berkeley neuroanatomist Marian Diamond points out, we reach our quantitative high point of brain cells well before we are even born?[5] All the way from birth through adolescence, we are losing cells and synapses, even as we learn more and more and our brains get bigger. How can that be?

A brain cell is like a telephone: There is no use having it unless it is wired up

Consider that a brain cell does not do any good unless it is connected to other brain cells so that it can send and receive information. What is going on during the early years of life, and even before that in the womb, is that superabundant brain cells are getting winnowed down through a cutthroat competition for connections.[6] If a cell fails to establish a connection, or enough connections with enough other cells, or if already-existing connections are not used, it dies. What determines whether connections are made? It is partly just a matter of some cells being defective in the first place, much as many of the sperm cells produced by a healthy adult male are defective and nonfunctional. It is also partly due to genetic pre-programming. But it is also a matter of which ones are needed.

It seems likely that we are better off if nature endows us with more brain cells than we could ever really use. The choice of which cells are then retained and which are killed off would depend on the demands of the environment. This kind of flexibility, or *plasticity*, would give us a distinct survival advantage. It enables our brains to be shaped by the needs we encounter in the world we are born into, rather than purely by some pre-set, fixed, evolutionarily determined blueprint.

So, instead of providing a fixed blueprint for all the 100 trillion or so connections between neurons, the brain comes laid out with the main "cable highways" and leaves the fine wiring to be determined by trial and error. If a newborn rat has its whiskers trimmed, the part of the cortex of its brain that decodes the whiskers' sensory input changes.[7] The connections that had been set up by the rat's genetic blueprint wither away, instead of developing complex branches. Plasticity can also be seen in the tiny protrusions on the neurons called *spines* and *filopodia*. These microscopic structures expand and contract on a minute-by-minute basis in response to sensory input. They work on a "use it or lose it" principle — if the input crossing a given synapse is not enough, it is pruned away.

A recent experiment with newborn ferrets shows that sensory input after birth can even cause an entire section of the brain to be recruited to perform a different function from the one normally housed there.[8,9] Ferrets, of course, can see and hear, and have different kinds of brain cells, in different regions of the cortex, specialized for each of these skills. But what happens if the nerve carrying auditory input from the ear is prevented from reaching the brain? In that case, the ferret's auditory brain regions (those that usually handle information coming from the ear) switch over to handling visual input, and develop specialized vision cells normally present only in the visual cortex. Then, the ferrets literally *see* with their auditory cortex. It is a remarkable illustration that, under the right conditions, even parts of the brain normally specialized for one function can develop to perform functions normally found only in different regions. This reorganization seems to be essentially the same kind that occurs in humans — even adults — who lose one of their senses.

What happens to us as we move through childhood is that our experience of the world is likewise determining what brain cells and synapses we really need. The ones we do not need are sloughed off. The ones we do need are retained — but not, of course, in their original state. They get *better* — which is why our brains grow, and why we know more, and can process more kinds of information more efficiently, at age 10 than age 1.

In the brain, quality is more important than quantity
The brain cells that are used develop better and thicker insulation — *myelin* — around their axon (the part that transmits information). Their dendrites (which receive information from other cells) multiply their branches. Dendritic branches sprout and the layering of myelin thickens which causes the brain to increase in size and weight all the way through mid-adolescence. Even though many cells and synapses have been weeded out by that age, those that remain are better developed and more efficient and effective for the skills and knowledge that have been acquired. So just remember: It is

not simply the *quantity* of brain cells that counts, but the *quality* — and the evidence suggests that high-quality brain cells are developed by *using* them.

Childhood is a particularly crucial "use it or lose it" time in our lives, because some skills — some aspects of language and vision, for example — have windows of opportunity known as "critical periods" that will close for good if those skills do not develop by the right age. But it is not just the classic critical period skills that are important to develop early in life. We all know that once someone learns how to ride a bike, they never really forget. They can get a little rusty, and reflexes may slow down, but they never have to go back to training wheels. Many other skills are, to varying degrees, like learning to ride a bike. It is not impossible to learn new skills later in life — how to drive with a stick shift, for example — but neural pathways begin to be laid down so they are available life long.

Here is where the concept of "neural hardwiring" gets a little blurred. It could be said that hardwiring is the designed-in circuitry, what humans are born with or genetically programmed to develop. But any skills, if learned and used early in life, may become so strongly wired into neural circuitry that they can be put to work as long as one is physically able.

So the "use-it-or-lose-it" idea has been proven for children. But what about adults?

While stimulation in childhood certainly adds to the ability to profit from experience later in life, an enriched environment improves performance throughout life. Experiments by Rosenzweig and Bennett have shown that rats weaned in an impoverished environment can catch up to the performance level of enriched-environment rats in solving spatial problems, once they have been given the same richness of exposure.[10] Other studies have shown that a bird's hippocampus — a seat of spatial memory — will grow when the bird is given food hiding-and-retrieving tasks well on in life, even if it was denied that experience when young.[11,12]

In fact, brain cells' dendrites grow — and shrink — throughout life, whether used or not. In the pioneering "enriched environment" experiments by Diamond, Rosenzweig, Bennett and colleagues at Berkeley, it was not just young rats that got bigger and better brains when they were placed in a varied, challenging, socially rich environment; old rats did too.[13] Not only did the old rats' dendritic branches proliferate or die back depending on the environment, the structure of the dendritic "spines" — the tiny contact points on the dendrites themselves — was amazingly sensitive to that environment.

Berkeley researcher James Connor found that the dendrites of rats who had been raised in an enriched environment had spines like bulbous lollipops, whereas "impoverished" rats had tiny nubs on their dendrites.[14] Other research with fish, honeybees, and humans has shown that experience interacts with the spines to alter their shape on an ongoing basis. The brain is not a static object after childhood, like a block of stone slowly worn down or chipped away with time; it is a collection of trillions of pieces — dendrites, spines, and synapses — that is in a constant state of flux and is constantly changing its size and shape as the brain interacts with the world around it.

Recent work has shown that, in fact, improved neuron quality may not be the only reason that brains can get bigger and better late in life. Two bodies of independent research reported in March 1999, from the Salk Institute in San Diego and Princeton University, add to other new evidence that adult animals do indeed grow new brain cells. (A Purdue researcher, Joseph Altman, actually offered evidence for this 35 years ago, but most scientists simply dismissed his findings at the time.[15])

Even more exciting are the factors that promote such growth. In the Salk study, mice that exercised regularly on a running wheel grew twice as many new brain cells as other mice.[16] The new cells appeared in the hippocampus, a part of the brain crucial for memory and learning. In the Princeton study, led by neuroscientist Elizabeth Gould, the apparent cause of the mice's doubled brain-cell growth was *mental* exercise.[17] Gould and her colleagues found that challenging mental tasks not only spurred the production of new hippocampal brain cells, but helped maintain existing ones as well. As Gould herself put it, "It's a classic case of 'use it or lose it'."

PRACTICAL WAYS TO APPLY RESULTS

The brains of laboratory animals are not alone in responding to enriched environments. A Swedish-American team led by the Salk Institute's Fred Gage recently found that, in fact, adult human brains can and do grow new neurons throughout life.[18] One reason so many animal studies are cited in brain research is that it is impractical to run experiments that allow a researcher to manipulate, at will, the life-long environment of humans. Also, many kinds of close structural analysis of the brain require techniques that can not be used with humans.

Scientists can find out more about the human brain in a variety of ways. One way is by dissecting the brains of people who elected to donate their organs to science after death. This approach can show up differences in the anatomy and physiology of the brain in

people with and without AD. Also, an increasingly sophisticated arsenal of scanning techniques is becoming available to watch a living brain at work without causing any harm. These methods include CAT, PET, fMRI, and SPECT. There is also a recent addition to this group of techniques, *transcranial magnetic stimulation* (TMS). This method goes beyond PET and fMRI because it can show a close temporal connection between brain activity and a given function.

Autopsies of AD patients' brains have shown that this disease appears as structural changes (plaques and tangles) among the neurons in certain parts of the cortex (the brain's outer layer) and hippocampus (a brain region involved in memory). It follows that as brain cells atrophy in those areas, those parts of the brain shrink. However, there is an inner ("intracranial") part of the skull that never shrinks, even if the brain within it does. It therefore reveals the high-water mark of brain size in that individual's life. A CAT scan study by Schofield et al. points to an inverse relationship between a person's peak brain size in life and the likelihood of their getting AD.[19] This evidence supports the theory that those who have built up a "functional reserve" of well-developed brain cells have a kind of built-in protection against AD. It may also explain why some people develop the characteristic structural signs of AD (plaques and tangles among the cells of some parts of the brain) without showing any signs of cognitive impairment.

As we have already seen, AD seems to be caused by a complex combination of factors, some genetic and others environmental. Some other degenerative diseases that affect the brain are more strongly genetically determined. Huntington's disease, for example — the disorder that felled songwriter Woody Guthrie — is caused by a dominant gene that is inherited at a 50% rate of probability by the offspring of someone with the disease. In other words, if the son or daughter of someone with Huntington's lives long enough, chances are 50-50 that he or she will get it too — regardless of general health, habits, or lifestyle. And if one of a pair of identical twins has Huntington's, chances are 100% that the twin sibling will get it too.

On the other hand, one of the twins can show more severe symptoms at a younger age than the other, and deteriorate more rapidly, suggesting that even with a genetically caused neurological disease, the course of progression of the disease can be influenced by the environment.

A very recent experiment by a team of Oxford researchers shows how the environment can have a powerful effect on the progression of a Huntington's-like disorder in mice.[20] The researchers raised half of a group of mice with a Huntington's-type gene in standard cages, and half in "environmentally enriched" cages filled with a constantly rotating collection of toys and games. Week by week, all the mice were tested on two separate tasks designed to reveal symptoms of the disease. The "standard-environment" mice showed symptoms earlier than "enriched-environment" mice in both tasks. In one task, only about half of the "enriched" mice had developed symptoms by the end of the experiment, while 100% of the "standard" mice had. In the other task, only one of 15 enriched mice showed symptoms by the end of the period compared, again, to 100% of the "standard" Huntington's mice.

Functional reserve and mental stimulation: How education and occupation may help protect you from AD

Many studies have pointed to the conclusion that the more education and the more challenging occupation one has, the less likely one is to get AD.[21,22,23,24] In fact, one statistical analysis of the results of several of these studies came to the conclusion that educational level is a stronger predictor of the likelihood of developing AD than any of the commonly cited factors, including family history of AD[25]

The problem, though, is that a correlation does not necessarily prove a cause. Educational level and occupation cluster with other lifestyle factors — exercise, diet, access to medical care, interests, consumption of alcohol and nicotine — that have an impact on many diseases, including dementia. That is why researchers always seek to control for additional factors by keeping them constant. One way to achieve this goal is to study only people who have the same lifestyle but different levels of education, or different occupations, and see who develops AD and who does not.

The most famous investigation of this type is what is often referred to as the Nun Study. This study, begun in 1991, has followed the cognitive health of 678 members of the School Sisters of Notre Dame congregation born before 1917. The nuns form a group with largely similar lifestyle variables, and several subsequent studies have drawn on carefully selected subgroups within the entire nun pool to investigate possible correlations between dementia and other factors that vary among the participants. All the participating nuns agreed in advance to allow their brains to be analyzed after death, so researchers have been able not only to analyze their cognitive function on an annual basis, but to identify structural signs of AD at autopsy.

One study that drew on the Nun Study data examined correlations between level of education and cognitive function among a subset of 247 of the nuns.[26] These nuns were carefully chosen for similar lifestyles, but differences in educational level. Remarkably, despite the equivalence in adult lifestyle, highly educated nuns were twice as likely to avoid AD and other dementias late in life than less educated nuns. This offers some proof that the "protective" effect of education early in life is not simply due to other lifestyle factors — diet, marriage status, occupation, or what have you — correlating with education level.

Even more striking findings were obtained in an investigation of the relation between writing style in early adult life and development of AD in old age among a subset of 93 nuns.[27] All 93 participants had submitted short autobiographies written after their religious training and before taking their vows, typically when they were in their early twenties. The authors of this study analyzed those early writing samples for "idea density" and "grammatical complexity" (see box, page 114). Those nuns who had written samples scoring low in these respects were more likely to have low

(Continued on page 116)

High Idea Density and Grammatical Complexity in Writing Style: A Sign of Low Risk for Alzheimer's?

"Idea density" is a measure of the average number of "ideas" per ten words. "Grammatical complexity" is graded according to how much embedding and syntactic subordination a sentence shows. Here is an excerpt comparing the nun who scored lowest in idea density and grammatical complexity (below left) with the nun who scored highest (below right). These are from autobiographical essays the nuns wrote when they were young adults, in their early twenties.

The sister who wrote the sample on the left died with Alzheimer's, while the one who wrote the sentence on the right was (at the time of the study) still alive with no cognitive impairment.

I was born in Eau Claire, Wis, on May 24, 1913 and was baptized in St James Church.	The happiest day of my life so far was my First Communion Day which was in June nineteen hundred and twenty when I was but eight years of age, and four years later in the same month I was confirmed by Bishop D.D. McGavick.

The researchers computed an idea density score of 3.9 and a grammatical complexity rating of 0 for the sentence excerpt on the left. The low grammatical complexity score reflects a simple one-clause sentence with no embedding. Here is how the idea density score was computed:

Idea 1: I was born
Idea 2: born in Eau Claire, Wis
Idea 3: born on May 24, 1913
Idea 4: I was baptized
Idea 5: was baptized in church
Idea 6: I was baptized in St. James Church
Idea 7: I was born and was baptized

Assuming 18 "words," seven ideas divided by 18 = 3.9. The sentence on the right was given an idea density score of 8.6, and a grammatical complexity rating of 7.

Sentences high in grammatical complexity impose more demands on working memory than ones low in grammatical complexity. A writing style high in grammatical complexity may reflect speech habits that impose frequent demands to exercise working memory skills.

To see how taxing embedding and subordination can be, try deciphering the made-up example below. This kind of sentence is in fact so difficult to decipher that, even though it does not violate any formal rules of grammar, any editor would rewrite it:

The fact that the kid told you about that I don't like you bothers me a lot.

(Translation: It bothers me a lot that the kid told you about the fact that I don't like you.)

You might say that the dense and complex sentence written by the nun who never got Alzheimer's is excessively wordy, while the simpler one is more straightforward and to the point. Hemingway painstakingly cultivated the latter type of writing style, while sentences from writers such as Proust and Faulkner are sometimes so long-winded and complicated as to be barely intelligible. You have got to admit, though, that reading Faulkner or Proust gives your working memory a better workout.

Compare these two samples:

Hemingway:

I wished her good night and went up-stairs. There were two letters and some papers. I looked at them under the gas-light in the dining-room. The letters were from the States. One was a bank statement. It showed a balance of $2432.60.

(Continued on page 116)

(Continued from page 115)

Faulkner:

There was a wisteria vine blooming for the second time
that summer on a wooden trellis before one window,
into which sparrows came now and then in random
gusts, making a dry vivid dusty sound before going
away: and opposite Quentin, Miss Coldfield in the eter-
nal black which she had worn for forty-three years now,
whether for sister, father, or nothusband none knew,
sitting so bolt upright in the straight hard chair that
was so tall for her that her legs hung straight and rigid
as if she had iron shinbones and ankles, clear of the
floor with that air of impotent and static rage like children's feet, and talking in that grim haggard amazed
voice until at last listening would renege and hearing-
sense self-confound and the long-dead object of her
impotent yet indomitable frustration would appear, as
though by outraged recapitulation evoked, quiet inat-
tentive and harmless, out of the biding and dreamy and
victorious dust.

(Continued from page 113)

cognitive test scores late in life, with low idea density
showing a stronger association with poor late-life cognitive performance than low grammatical complexity. The
most striking finding, though, was that the nuns with
low idea density early in life developed AD in old age,
while not a single one with high idea density did so.

These studies, then, show that low education and (by a
certain measure) simple linguistic style early in life are
risk factors for developing Alzheimer's and other
dementias in old age. Why?

One interpretation of these findings is that experiences and habits from childhood to early adulthood help to build up a "cognitive reserve" or "brain reserve capacity" that can be drawn on later in life.[28] That is, extra, more richly developed neural pathways laid down early in life can give the aging brain more of a reserve to draw on, even if some neurons die or become less efficient.

Another theory — perfectly compatible with the one just described — holds that some of the protective effect of education and "idea density" in writing against Alzheimer's comes from the role of mental exercise in keeping neurons alive and healthy.[29] That is, education may help lay the groundwork for lifelong patterns of intellectually challenging activities, and "idea density" in young-adult writing style may predict lasting habits of processing complex linguistic structures. Just as physical exercise boosts blood and oxygen to the body as a whole, mental exercise increases the supply of blood-borne nutrients to the brain. Ample nutrients help ward off the brain-toxic effects of the glucocorticoid "stress" hormone and may also serve to protect against free radicals (see Chapter 3). Also, increased brain work stimulates DNA repair of brain cells.

Support for the role of the protective effect of education against AD also comes from brain-scan studies. For example, among Alzheimer's patients with equivalent degrees of disease severity, blood flow to Alzheimer's-affected regions of the brain is lower in patients with more advanced education.[30] Given that reduced blood flow is a physical symptom of AD, this means that, on a physical level, the well-educated patients had more severe AD than the others — and yet, in their cognitive ability they showed no more signs of the disease than the poorly-educated patients with less-severe brain-scan symptoms. So it may be that structural effects of AD in the brain — plaques and tangles, neuron loss, reduced blood flow — may be partially overcome by a greater reserve of neurons, synapses, and pathways built up over a lifetime of mental stimulation.

Lifelong patterns of stimulating activities and interests may be as important as early education in helping to forestall dementia. Evidence for this comes from studies that show a strong relation between occupation and risk of dementia. An influential French study showed that the risk of dementia among laborers in Bordeaux is *two to three times* greater than among professionals.[31] Occupational status is in fact a far more important variable than education alone. The preventive effect of varied and mentally challenging occupations on Alzheimer's has been confirmed in many other studies in the last decade, in the U.S., Italy, and Israel.[32,33]

Detecting a lively mind in the brain

Researchers Jacobs, Schall, and Scheibel have discovered what the protective effects of an enriched life might look like in the brain.[34] The first branching split of a dendrite is called "first-order," the second level "second-order," and so on. In postmortem analyses of Wernicke's area (a part of the brain used in language), they found that the higher the educational level, the more higher-level branching (fourth-level and above) there was in that part of that person's brain.

One of the most important studies for the application of

the "use it or lose it" concept to successful aging is reported by Schaie (1994).[35] He followed the lives of over 5,000 adults for a period of up to 35 years, and revealed several variables that may lower the risk of cognitive decline in old age. One is a cluster of factors including above-average education and occupations that involve work that is high in complexity and low in routine. Another cluster of factors includes interesting hobbies and leisure pursuits. All these factors usually will involve complex and intellectually stimulating environments. Examples might be extensive reading, travel, going to cultural events, pursuing continuing education, and participation in clubs and professional associations.

All these studies point to an important conclusion. The human brains is not so much like the knees of a baseball catcher as like the heart of a runner. On the theory that every heart has a pre-set number of beats before it wears out, exercise that accelerates heart rate might be thought to accelerate death. But that is not the way it really works. Using the heart strengthens it, lengthens its life, and improves the overall quality of life of the body that houses it. All the current evidence from experimental studies is showing that this is the way our brains work as well. We should make a constant effort to keep our brains active and challenged, in order to keep them as healthy as a runner keeps his or her heart.

How to enrich your own environment: Curiosity does *not* kill the cat, it makes the cat smarter

Over 30 years ago, Alan Hein made a point that is still crucially important for those of us interested in "optimal aging."[36] He designed an ingenious experiment that looked at how the visual system of the cat develops. The experiment showed that only certain sorts of environmental stimulation will lead to the development of more acute visual processing centers in kittens' brains. The critical thing the experiment showed was that proper development only happens when the stimulation results from *active* exploration, as opposed to purely passive exposure. The two kittens were linked by a carousel-like contraption that allowed one kitten to explore freely while the other could not. Every time the active kitten moved towards an interesting visual stimulus, the passive one would be automatically swiveled towards an equivalent object or image. In this way, both kittens were exposed to the same visual environment, but only one did so in an active manner. When the brains of the cats were eventually examined, only the cat who had explored the environment actively had developed a brain that had superior visual processing abilities. This study indicates the human will must be determined to build a better brain, or maintain the powers it has already acquired. A janitor in the Library of Congress does not acquire an encyclopedic knowledge merely by being in the presence of so many books. Like a kitten, the brain likes to explore and interact with the learning resources that are available to it. That early curiosity will have a positive effect on its health in the future.

COMMON SUBSTANCES IN THE BODY THAT MAY HELP THE BRAIN

**What the near future holds:
The promise of stem cells**

One of the most exciting new avenues of treatment for brain diseases, including AD, has grown out of recent experiments with *stem cells.* These are general-purpose cells that can divide and differentiate to produce specialist cells, including brain cells. Some scientists see stem cells as a source of treatment for brain damage and degenerative brain diseases.

When a human egg is first fertilized by a sperm, it becomes a single cell from which all cells of the body-to-be will be created. This "mother of all stem cells" is what biologists call *totipotent,* meaning that it has unlimited creative capacity. One level down from the totipotent "mother" stem cell are *pluripotent* cells, capable of generating all the cells of the body (but not the placenta) that the fetus needs to survive. By a process of division and specialization, further levels of stem cells are created, leading ultimately to each particular cell — blood, brain, skin, etc. — of the body.

Some of the more specialized stem cells continue to exist in the body after birth — indeed, throughout life. Blood stem cells, for example, generate new red blood cells, white blood cells, and platelets *ad infinitum.* They cannot generate all the cells types in the body — they are not totipotent or pluripotent — but they are still *multipotent,* capable of generating a number of different specific cells of a general type.

Do adult human brains have stem cells?

Until very recently, the accepted wisdom has been that we carry no stem cells for the brain into adulthood — that, in other words, central nervous system cells in the brain and spine cannot regenerate the way that the cells in our skin, blood, and other body systems do. As with so much other long-accepted knowledge about the brain, this postulate turns out to be wrong.

There is a chemical called *bromodoxyuredine* (BrdU), which is used as a kind of marker to pinpoint rapid cell division, as happens most dramatically when healthy cells turn cancerous. In 1998, Fred Gage of the Salk Institute performed autopsies on several terminal cancer patients who had been injected with the chemical, and found BrdU in their brains.[37] This was evidence that their brain cells were dividing and regenerating brain cells. Other studies since then have shown the ongoing regeneration of neurons — *neurogenesis* — in the brains of adult animals, including primates closely related to humans. Recently, a group of researchers at Sweden's Karolinska Institute demonstrated that the adult human brain carries stem cells as well.[38]

Human brain stem cell research is proceeding at a breathtaking pace. In only a few months after researchers became aware of their existence, the scientific community discovered a great deal about them. For one thing, stem cells reside quietly near the brain *ventricles* (fluid-filled structures in the brain's interior) until spurred into action by growth factors. They can then develop into either of the two most general classes of brain cell, neurons or *glial cells*. (Glial cells are a special type of cell that researchers have only recently come to treat with the respect they deserve; formerly thought to provide little more than a structural "glue" for neurons, it turns out they manufacture and store substances essential to the survival and health of the neurons.) When someone suffers a stroke or other brain injury, the stem cells are switched from their usual resting state into the production of specialized brain cells that migrate to the injury site. And most bizarrely of all, when brain stem cells are taken from mice and injected into the tails of other mice, they develop into blood cells![39,40] The mechanism for this effect is not clear, but there must be something in that part of the mouse's body — specific growth factors, perhaps — that can move even a stem cell from a different body system into becoming a blood cell. Suffice it to say that brain stem cells are still somewhat mysterious, but clearly have tremendous potential for brain maintenance and repair. They are like money in the savings account of a pensioner, spent only in small amounts except in case of emergency. It would be nice, of course, to figure out how to have more of those precious funds to draw on.

Hi-tech ways to boost brain stem cell activity

One of the most controversial aspects of stem cell research has to do with the harvesting of pluripotent stem cells from aborted human fetuses. The hope is that such cells may be coaxed into generating several kinds of more specialized cells, and then implanted into the body or brain or a person with a disease of a corresponding cell or organ type, such as diabetes (pancreatic cells), heart disease (heart cells), or Parkinson's or Alzheimer's (brain cells). This "coaxing" is a matter of switching on the right genes in the stem cell that trigger development into just the right kind of more specialized cell. Recent evidence indicates that this result may be accomplished by identifying the appropriate growth factor (see below) that spurs the cell in the desired direction. An even simpler technique would be to extract fetal tissue that has already become specialized in the right direction. This kind of experiment has in fact already been successfully performed by a Swedish team led by Anders Bjorklund, who implanted fetal brain cells into the brains of Parkinson's patients.[41]

Another promising avenue of current research is the manipulation of a patient's own stem cells into generating brain cells of the right type, an approach that avoids the politically and socially controversial issue of harvesting fetal tissue. It also avoids the medically critical problem of rejection of implants by the recipient's immune system.

Making the brain work strengthens its power
It is important to remember, though, that even with a procedure as invasive as fetal implants, the "use it or lose it" doctrine still applies — just as it does to newborns. In other words, if implanted cells are not used for the purpose for which they are implanted, they will die. A well-functioning mind develops out of an intricate interplay between biological endowment and life experience. An infant given all the brain cells in the universe will not develop a good mind unless those neurons are linked up and enlarged through an active exploration of the environment. The same principle applies, as well, to an adult

recipient of stem cells. In animal models, when implants are combined with a program of mental stimulation, they stand a much better chance of success than the implants alone.[42,43]

The upshot of the profusion of advice and research findings reported on a daily basis in the medical journals and the media is that many factors influence healthy brain development and aging, and one cannot expect to find a single magic bullet. But no matter what, brain-cell development, maintenance, and repair are guided by the uses to which we put our minds, both in childhood or adulthood.

The brain's own miracle cure: Nerve growth factors

What about the idea of keeping the *old* brain cells in good working order? Here is where we all need to pay attention to the research about combatting neuron-destroying substances such as glucocorticoids, beta-amyloid proteins, and free radicals (see Chapter 3). This domain is also where the brain's self-support system comes in, especially the brain's own substances for keeping neurons healthy. The most intensive research in this area involves the class of brain molecules called *nerve growth factors*.

For many years, brain researchers have understood that the creation and survival of brain cells may hinge on nerve growth factors. Growth factors, including *neurotrophic* brain proteins, are biochemical compounds that switch on the genes of stem cells so they develop into the type of cell the brain requires. They then help to guide those newly generated cells to the appropriate part of the brain. Finally, they help maintain, protect, and repair brain cells once they are in place.

Ramón y Cajal, the pioneering brain researcher with pessimistic views about the possibility of neurogenesis in the adult central nervous system, conjectured that the problem with adults may be an absence of the growth factors so abundant in the developing brain of a fetus. It turns out that adult brains do, indeed, produce growth factors and that these chemicals continue to play a role in brain cell maintenance and repair throughout life. Recent research has focused on identifying the different kinds of growth factor involved in maintaining different kinds of brain cell, and in learning how to manipulate or augment the brain's own growth factors to keep brain cells alive and healthy.

One important finding is that the brain produces extra quantities — five to 50 times normal levels — of growth factors after a brain injury.[44] Also, it has been discovered that glial cells — those traditionally underrated brain cells that help neurons to function properly — produce growth factors essential to the survival of neurons, and migrate to the site of a brain injury immediately after it occurs.[45]

This evidence suggests the possibility that we could help stroke or head-accident victims recover more quickly by stimulating the brain's production of growth factors, or by somehow adding to what the brain is already doing to help itself. One line of current research is in fact exploring the feasibility of injecting growth factors into the site of a brain injury to help the brain recover more quickly.[46] In animal experiments, even neurons apparently destroyed by having their axons cut (rendering them incapable of sending messages to other brain cells) are restored to full function if nerve growth factors are injected up to three weeks after the damage.[47]

Other experiments have shown that aged rats can regain youthful learning curves when growth factors are injected into the same frontal regions of the brain that degenerate in AD.[48] Recently, researchers have also successfully grafted cells into rats that secrete growth factors on an ongoing basis, to *prevent* cognitive impairment before it even starts.[49]

In the meantime, the news that counts in real-world situations is this: The "use it or lose it" principle applies to growth factors as well as to the regeneration of neurons. In fact, raised levels of growth factors may be the reason that an enriched environment enhances survival of newly generated brain cells, aids in recovery from stroke, and helps forestall dementias such as Alzheimer's.

It has been known for many years that an enriched environment — one providing extra physical, social, and mental stimulation — translates into improved performance on intelligence-type tests and into a bigger brain. In her pioneering studies, Marian Diamond attributed the larger brains of enriched-environment rats to larger neurons with richer-branching axons and dendrites and thicker myelin insulation. Later work found evidence for a larger number of neurons in an "enriched" brain as well, and evidence for a doubled rate of new brain-cell production under enriched conditions.

Over the last ten years, a substantial body of research has shown that the environment also has a strong effect on those all-important brain nutrients known as nerve growth factors, starting with a 1990 study that revealed high levels of nerve growth factors in enriched-environment rats compared to standard-environment ones.[50,51,52]

These findings are important for those worried about declines in learning ability and memory, because the hippocampus is a brain structure central to those skills; it is also one of the brain structures most strongly affected by AD. A subsequent study showed that rats with free access to a running wheel had increased levels of a neurotrophic-type growth factor than rats that had no chance to exercise.[53] In this experiment, too, the extra growth factor molecules showed up in the hippocampus. Recent studies have proven that exercise increases growth factor levels in older men and women.[54,55] So we now have proof that the findings about the relationship between an enriched environment and nerve growth factor levels in the brain apply to humans too.

FOOTNOTES FOR SECTION IV

[1]Peter S. Eriksson et al. (1998). Neurogenesis in the adult human hippocampus. Nature Medicine 4/11:1313-17.

[2]C.B. Johansson et al. (1999). Neural stem cells in the adult human brain. Experimental Cell Research 253/2:733-6.

[3]David F. Swaab (1991). Brain aging and Alzheimer's disease, "wear and tear" versus "use it or lose it." Neurobiology of Aging 12:317-24.

[4]David S. Swaab (1998). Reduced neuronal activity and reactivation in Alzheimer's disease. Progress in Brain Research 117:343-77.

[5]Marian Diamond and Janet Hopson (1998). Magic Trees of the Mind: How to nurture your child's intelligence, creativity, and healthy emotions from birth through adolescence. New York: Plume.

[6]Gerald M. Edelman (1987). Neural Darwinism: The theory of neuronal group selection. New York: Basic Books.

[7]Balazs Lendvai et al. (2000). Experience-dependent plasticity of dendritic spines in the developing rat barrel cortex in vivo. Nature 404:876-81.

[8]Laurie von Melchner, Sarah L. Pallas, and Mriganka Sur (2000). Visual behavior mediated by retinal projections directed to the auditory pathway. Nature 404:871-5.

[9]Jitendra Sharma, Alessandra Angelucci, and Mriganka Sur (2000). Induction of visual orientation modules in auditory cortex. Nature 404:841-7.

[10]Mark R. Rosenzweig and Edward L. Bennett (1996). Psychobiology of plasticity: effects of training and experience on brain and behavior. Behavioural Brain Research 78:57-65.

[11]Nicky S. Clayton and John R. Krebs (1994). Hippocampal growth and attrition in birds affected by experience. Proceedings of the National Academy of Science USA 91:7410-14.

[12]C. Scharff et al. (2000). Targeted neuronal death affects neuronal replacement and vocal behavior in adult songbirds. Neuron 25:481-92.

[13]E.L. Bennett et al. (1974). Effects of successive environments on brain measures. Physiology and Behavior 12/4:621-31.

[14]James R. Connor and Marian C. Diamond (1982). A comparison of dendritic spine number and type on pyramidal neurons of the visual cortex of old rats from social or isolated environments. The Journal of Comparative Neurology 210:99-106.

[15]Joseph Altman and Gopal D. Das (1965). Autoradiographic and histological evidence of postnatal hippocampal neurogenesis in rats. Journal of Comparative Neurology 124:319-36.

[16]Henriette van Praag, Gerd Kempermann, and Fred H. Gage (1999). Running increases cell proliferation and neurogenesis in the adult mouse dentate gyrus. Nature Neuroscience 2/3:266-70.

[17]Elizabeth Gould et l. (1999). Learning enhances adult neurogenesis in the hippocampal formation. Nature Neuroscience 2/3:260-5.

[18]Peter S. Eriksson et al. (1998). Neurogenesis in the adult human hippocampus. Nature Medicine 4/11:1313-17.

[19]Peter W. Schofield et al. (1995). The age at onset of Alzheimer's disease and an intracranial area measurement: a relationship. Archives of Neurology 52:95-8.

[20]Anton van Dellen et al. (2000). Delaying the onset of Huntington's in mice. Nature 404:721-2.

[21]Yaakov Stern et al. (1994). Influence of education and occupation on the incidence of Alzheimer's disease. Journal of the American Medical Association 271/13:1004-10.

[22]Robert P. Freidland (1993). Epidemiology, education, and the ecology of Alzheimer's disease. Neurology 43:246-9.

[23]Margaret Gatz et al. (1994). Dementia: not just a search for the gene. The Gerontologist 34/2:251-5.

[24]I. Raiha et al. (1998). Environmental differences in twin pairs discordant for Alzheimer's disease. Journal of Neurology, Neurosurgery, and Psychiatry 65/5:785-7.

[25]James A. Mortimer and Amy B. Graves (1993). Education and other socioeconomic determinants of dementia and Alzheimer's disease. Neurology 43 (Suppl. 4):S39-44.

[26]David A. Snowdon et al. (1989). Years of life with good and poor mental function in the elderly. Journal of Clinical Epidemiology 42:1055-66.

[27]David A. Snowdon et al. (1996). Linguistic ability in early life and cognitive function and Alzheimer's disease in late life. Journal of the American Medical Association 275/7:528-32.

[28]Yaakov Stern et al. (1994). Influence of education and occupation on the incidence of Alzheimer's disease. Journal of the American Medical Association 271/13:1004-10.

[29]Robert P. Freidland (1993). Epidemiology, education, and the ecology of Alzheimer's disease. Neurology 43:246-9.

[30]Yaakov Stern et al. (1992). Inverse relationship between education and parietotemporal perfusion deficit in Alzheimer's disease. Annals of Neurology 32/3:371-5.

[31]J.F. Dartigues et al. (1992). Occupation during life and memory performance in nondemented French elderly community residents. Neurology 42:1697-1701.

[32]A.D. Korczyn, E. Kahana, and Y. Galper (1991). Epidemiology of dementia in Ashkelon, Israel. Neuroepidemiology 10:100.

[33]S. Bonaiuto, E. Rocca, and A. Lippi (1990). Impact of education and occupation on the prevalence of Alzheimer's disease (AD) and multi-infarct dementia in Macerata Province, Italy. Neurology 40 (Suppl. 1):346.

[34]Bob Jacobs, Matthew Schall, and Arnold B. Scheibel (1993). A quantitative dendritic analysis of Wernicke's area in humans. The Journal of Comparative Neurology 327:97-111.

[35]K.W. Schaie (1994). The course of adult intellectual development. American Psychologist 49:304-13.

[36]Richard Held (1965). Plasticity in sensory motor systems. Scientific American 213:84-94.

[37]Peter S. Eriksson et al. (1998). Neurogenesis in the adult human hippocampus. Nature Medicine 4/11:1313-17.

[38]C.B. Johansson et al. (1999). Neural stem cells in the adult human brain. Experimental Cell Research 253/2:733-6.

[39]Anders Bjorklund and Clive Svendsen (1999). Breaking the brain-blood barrier. Nature 397:569-70.

[40]C.R. Bjornson et al. (1999). Turning brain into blood: a hematopoietic fate adopted by adult neural stem cells in vivo. Science 283:534-537.

[41]C. Rosenblad, D.K. Kirik, and Anders Bjorklund (2000). Sequential administration of GDNF into the substantia nigra and striatum. Experimental Neurology 61/2:503-16.

[42]C. Kelche et al. (1995). The effects of intrahippocampal grafts, training, and postoperative housing on behavioral recovery after septohippocampal damage in the rat. Neurobiology of Learning and Memory 63/2:155-66.

[43]Donald G. Stein, Simon Brailowsky, and Bruno Will (1997). Brain Repair. Oxford: Oxford University Press.

[44]Donald G. Stein, Simon Brailowsky, and Bruno Will (1997). Brain Repair. Oxford: Oxford University Press.

[45]Donald G. Stein, Simon Brailowsky, and Bruno Will (1997). Brain Repair. Oxford: Oxford University Press.

[46]Grant Sinson, Madhu Voddi, and Tracy K. McIntosh (1995). Nerve growth factor administration attenuates cognitive but not neurobehavioral motor dysfunction or hippocampal cell loss following fluid-percussion brain injury in rats. Journal of Neurochemistry 65/5:2209-16.

[47]Donald G. Stein, Simon Brailowsky, and Bruno Will (1997). Brain Repair. Oxford: Oxford University Press.

[48]W. Fischer et al. (1991). NGF improves spatial memory in aged rodents as a function of age. Journal of Neuroscience 11/7:1889-1906.

[49]Alberto Martinez-Serrano and Anders Bjorklund (1998). Ex vivo nerve growth factor gene transfer to the basal forebrain in presymptomatic middle-aged rats prevents the development of cholinergic neuron atrophy during aging. Proceedings of the National Academy of Science USA 95:1858-63.

[50]F. Gomez-Pinilla, V. So, and S.P Kesslak (1998). Spatial learning and physical activity contribute to the induction of fibroblast growth factor: neural substrates for increased cognition associated with exercise. Neuroscience 85/1:53-61.

[51]T.M. Pham et al. (1999). Effects of environmental enrichment on cognitive function and hippocampal NGF in the brains of non-handled rats. Behavioural Brain Research 103/1:63-70.

[52]A.K. Mohammed et al. (1990). Environmental influence on behavior and nerve growth factor in the brain. Brain Research 528/1:62-70.

[53]S.A. Neeper et al. (1995). Exercise and brain neurotrophins. Nature 375:109.

[54]S. Bermon et al. (1999). Responses of total and free insulin-like growth factor-1 and insulin-like growth factor binding protein-3 after resistance exercise and training in elderly subjects. Acta Physiologica Scandinavica 165/1:51-6.

[55]S.G. Chadan et al. (1999). Influence of physical activity on plasma insulin-like growth factor-1and insulin-like growth factor binding proteins in healthy older women. Mechanisms of Ageing and Development 109/1:21-34.

SECTION V
CONDITIONING EXERCISES

TARGETED TO SPECIFIC BRAIN FUNCTIONS THAT ARE AT RISK WITH AGING

The text accompanying each of the following six mental exercises suggests tactical approaches and notes some of the systems in the brain that are stimulated while attempting to solve each of them. The optional Hint printed upside down below each exercise is intended to break up any cases of mental block that might have set in as each task is confronted. See page 143 for solutions.

DIGI-CLUE

Here's a puzzle to help you practice your "executive" pattern-abstracting abilities. The trick here is to play with the numbers in a completed row until a relationship emerges among them. When you think you might have it, test your hypothesis against another row with all the numbers filled in. This is a classic left-hemisphere logic exercise, although you do have to hit on a little leap of insight to get the right answer.

2	1	8	1	3
3	8	7	2	9
1	1	1	1	0
4	5	6	3	9
5	5	9		6

(**Hint:** Try adding two of the numbers together to get a sum, and compare that sum to the sum of two other numbers in the same row.)

These two mental tasks are trickier than you might think, because you don't know what to look for. All you know is that you have to find some recurring element or other. In the Double-Up task you must look for two of the same letters; in the Digi-Tally task, a recurring group of numbers. It would take far too long to check each element (letter or number-group) one by one against each of the others, so you have to rely on your executive skills to figure out a strategy for quickly finding the recur-

DOUBLE-UP

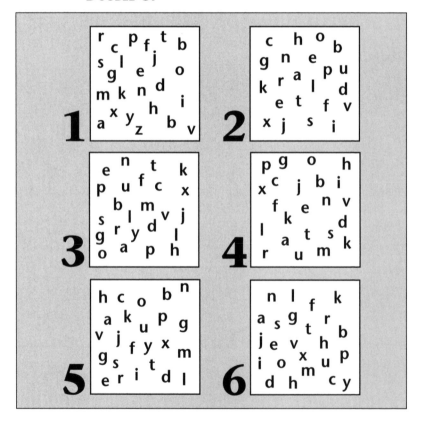

(**Hint:** For each group, instead of focusing on each letter in turn, try scanning the whole box for similar-looking shapes.)

ring element. Both of these puzzles feature numbers and letters, symbols that the left hemisphere excels in manipulating. However, to solve most problems the human brain engages many tools. For example, in this task, using the right hemisphere of the brain to visually scan the symbols as spatial shapes will probably yield a faster result. The Double-Up task also tests your ability to avoid interference effects (see page 36), so that your letter search in each box is not influenced by your choice from a previous box.

DIGIT-TALLY

a	2 6 1 0 4 1 7	**k**	1 6 0 3 5 3 6
b	8 3 7 1 9 4 5	**l**	2 7 1 7 4 6 9
c	1 8 3 1 5 2 7	**m**	4 1 7 3 9 5 8
d	5 7 0 1 2 5 8	**n**	3 6 9 1 6 2 1
e	1 2 3 2 4 3 1	**o**	1 8 2 7 7 7 5
f	8 1 4 9 5 3 7	**p**	3 0 1 0 5 1 2
g	9 2 3 1 3 4 9	**q**	2 1 9 4 9 8 4
h	1 5 8 4 8 6 8	**r**	5 3 7 1 9 4 8
i	5 3 7 9 8 1 4	**s**	1 6 8 3 8 9 0
j	7 3 1 3 2 5 0	**t**	4 0 2 1 5 0 3

(**Hint:** There is only one recurring sequence of numbers, so once you find what it is you can quickly run through the rest of the list to locate it wherever it recurs.)

SPOKESAMATICIAN

This task is reminiscent of classical number puzzles known as "magic squares". What makes the square magic (there are also magic triangles, stars, and other shapes), all the numbers in the grid must add up to the same sum total in any direction. Two general types of mental activity are heavily taxed in this sort of puzzle. First, it is essential to do the math correctly so that the numbers in each line or arc add up to the desired total (219). On the other hand, you need to grasp the logic and balance of the entire puzzle as an interlocking, multidimensional whole. Each number participates in at least two lines or arcs, which in turn contain other numbers participating in other lines or arcs. If you allow your mind's eye to be too myopic — focus-

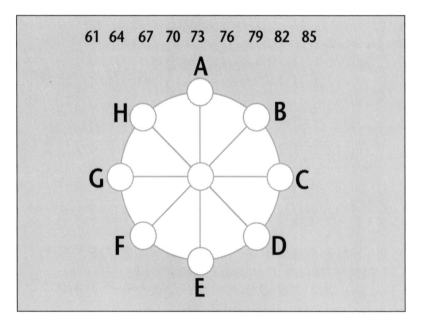

61 64 67 70 73 76 79 82 85

A
H
B
G
C
F
D
E

(**Hint:** The number you place in the center is the one that will have to join the greatest number of sequences with other numbers. The one that can be added to the greatest number of other pairs to add up to the desired total (219) is the one in the exact middle of the series — 73. So place that one in the center. From there on, keep in mind that every high number in the wheel must be counterbalanced by a low number placed opposite from it.)

ing only on each number, or even just on a single line or arc of numbers — you will burden your powers of concentration with an interminable, tedious, trial-and-error task. What you must do, then, is tap your executive skills to devise a strategy that relies more heavily on a parallel processing, multidimensional, "holistic" mode of thinking which draws on right-hemisphere abilities. In this task many regions of the brain must be brought to bear to meet the challenge.

COINTEST

This mental task helps you to exercise your executive skills (see Chapter 2), because you'll have to plan and think ahead to devise an effective strategy to get the coins into the correct sequence in the least number of moves. You'll also be relying on your mental scratch pad, a component of working memory that allows you to hold a visual image in your mind's eye while you manipulate it or proceed to other steps of the problem. The challenge of visualizing moves before making them engages spatial skills, a specialized ability of the right hemisphere, more heavily than most logic puzzles. To push the limits of your scratch pad memory, try working all the way through to a solution in your head without moving any actual coins with your hand.

accordingly.)

(**Hint:** It's OK to move coins so that there are gaps in the row. On your first move, keep in mind that your goal is to get the dimes on the left relative to the quarters. Choose your first pair of coins

WORD WHEEL

The format of this task is similar to a crossword puzzle. The main difference is that the answers overlap rather than intersect. It challenges your brain's ability to retrieve appropriate words from its associative memory — a skill many people feel they have trouble with as they get older — as well as activating other left-brain language skills. Unlike some of the other tasks that require parallel processing, the solution to this task reveals itself by proceeding in a simple, linear fashion from one answer to the next, until the circle is completely filled in with correctly overlapping words.

Just as one word leads to another, words lead into each other, or overlap. If you start with the right word written in clockwise from slot number 1, you should have little trouble completing the circle with nine additional overlapping words. Each word starts in a numbered slot that corresponds to the number of the clue.

Par is 5 minutes.

Clues:

1. Cheese tool
2. Succinct
3. Arcane
4. When drawing a pension
5. False clue
6. Circus employee
7. Camper's fuel
8. Seeing
9. Hockey boo-boo
10. Thankless person

(**Hint:** Clue number five is two words, referring to a fish of a different color.)

Index

acetylcholine, 89
aging, 11
  and Alzheimer's disease, 19-22
  and memory, 20, 30, 40, 42, 46-49
  normal, 19, 21-22
  protecting against effects of, 67-68
  and reaction time, 29-31
alcohol, and dementia, 80
Altman, Joseph, 108
Alzheimer, Alois, 22
Alzheimer's disease (AD)
  antioxidant therapy for, 84-85
  brain changes in, 110
  brain disuse and, 102-103
  causes of, 94-95
  cholinergic system and, 86-87, 89
  drug therapy for, 90
  DSM-IV diagnostic criteria for, 13
  educational level and, 112-118
  environment and, 112, 119
  free radicals and, 24
  genetics of, 22-23, 90-92
  incidence of, 11, 21
  risk factors for, 19, 22-23
  screening tests for, 16, 76-78
  signs of, 13, 17, 18, 19-20
  twin studies of, 23.
  See also Dementia
amygdala, 26
antioxidants
  to combat free radical damage,
    24, 83-85
  production in brain, 102
apolipoprotein E, 91-92
APP (protein), 83, 91
Aricept, 90
attention, divided, 37-38
axons, 26, 105

behavior, changes in Alzheimer's
  disease, 21
beta-amyloid, 83
Bjorklund, Anders, 124
brain
  activity as benefit to, 11, 24-25,
    101, 102, 106, 117
  in adulthood, 107-108

anatomy of, 26
changes in Alzheimer's, 110
in childhood, 106
cholinergic system of, 86-87
development of, 105-106
frontal lobe of, 33, 35, 38-39, 51
genetic diseases of, 110-111
illustrated, 26
interconnectivity in, 103-105
localization in, 99
neurogenesis in, 122-128
outmoded beliefs about, 98-99
redundancy in, 99-100
substances beneficial to, 125-128
substances damaging to, 25, 82-
  83, 101-102
ventricles of, 122-123
bromodoxyuridine (BrdU), 122

Cajal, Ramón y, 98, 126
cats, visual system of, 120
cholinergic system, 86-87, 89
cholinesterase inhibitors, to treat
  Alzheimer's disease, 84
cingulate gyrus, 26
circadian clock, regulation of, 85
cognitive difficulties
  in Alzheimer's disease, 21
  causes of, 74-75, 79-80
Connor, James, 107
convergent thinking, 66
corpus callosum, 26
cortex
  anatomy of, 26
  and memory, 32, 33
cortisol, 87

delayed recall, tests of, 76-78
dementia
  alcohol and, 80
  depression and, 25
  differential diagnosis of, 18-19
  distinguished from depression,
    19, 74-75
  estrogens to counteract, 86-87
  incidence of, 29
  mini-strokes as cause of, 80

screening test for, 17
as side effect of medication, 79-80
stress and, 25
warning signs of, 19, 20-21.
See also Alzheimer's disease
dendrites, 26, 105
    development of, 107
    level of branching of, 118-119
depression
    and dementia, 25
    distinguished from dementia, 19, 74-75
    lifestyle issues in, 75, 77
    as risk factor for dementia, 75
Diamond, Marian, 103, 127
disorientation, in Alzheimer's disease, 20
distractedness, normality of, 20
divergent thinking, 66-67
divided attention, 37-38
Donepezil, 90

education, and Alzheimer's, 112-118
Einstellung, 60, 64, 65
encoding, 50
    elaborative, 52-53
environmental enrichment, 24-25, 80
    active exploration in, 120
    health benefits of, 111-112
    and neuronal growth, 127
estrogen replacement therapy, 86
executive skills, 34
Exelon, 90

ferrets, 104-105
filopodia, of neuron, 104
flexibility
    brain plasticity, 104
    mental, 58, 65-67
forgetfulness, in Alzheimer's disease, 20
free radicals, brain damage caused by, 24, 82-83, 101
frontal lobe, 26

effects of damage to, 35
functions of, 33, 38-39, 51

Gage, Fred, 109, 122
genes
    and Alzheimer's disease, 22-23, 90-92
    role in mental development, 11, 23-24
ginkgo biloba, 84-85
glial cells, 39, 123
    nerve growth factor production by, 126
glucocorticoids, effects on brain, 101-102
Gould, Elizabeth, 108
gray matter, 39
growth factors, 82
Guthrie, Woody, 110

Hein, Alan, 120
hemispherectomy, 99
hippocampus, 26
    Alzheimer's disease and, 128
    growth of, 108, 128
    and memory, 32, 33, 107
Huntington's chorea, 110-111
    environment and, 111-112
hypothalamus, 26

infarct, defined, 80
intelligence, divergent, 66-67
interference, 36
    proactive, 36
    retroactive, 37
IQ tests, weaknesses of, 65

Jar Game, 62-65
judgment problems, in Alzheimer's disease, 20

language impairment, in Alzheimer's disease, 20
limbic system, illustrated, 26
long-term memory, 32

melatonin, functions of, 85-86

memory
aids to, 52-58, 65-67
cortex and, 32, 33
dementia-related loss of, 20
and executive skills, 48-52
facets of, 31
frontal lobes and, 33, 38-39, 51
hippocampus and, 32, 33
interference with, 36-37
long-term, 32
mental flexibility and, 58-60, 65-67
normal loss with aging, 20, 30-31
short-term, 32, 34-35
source, 33
tricks to help, 52-55
visual working, 42, 46-47
working, 33-34
memory span test, 37
mental acuity, tests of, 14-17
mental flexibility, 58-60, 65-67
Metrifonate, 90
Mini-Mental State Examination, 14
mini-strokes, causing dementia, 80
misplacing objects, in Alzheimer's disease, 21
mnemonics, 53, 55
use of, 56
mood
changes in Alzheimer's disease, 21
as contributory factor to dementia, 25
multi-infarct dementia, 80
multipotency, defined, 121-122
myelin, 105

names, remembering, 54
nerve growth factors, 125
production of, 126-127
neurogenesis, 122
neuron(s)
aging and, 30
exercise and, 108, 117, 127
illustrated, 26
interconnectivity of, 103-105
structure of, 104

Nun study (of Alzheimer's), 113-117

occipital lobe, 26
occupation, and Alzheimer's, 112
olfactory bulb, 26 [ed: please note typo in text]
oxygen, overdose of, 102

paired associate learning, 40
tests of, 41, 43
parietal lobe, 26
Parkinson's disease, stem-cell treatment of, 124
perseveration, 60
personality, changes in Alzheimer's disease, 21
phrenology, 98
plaque, 83
plasticity, 104
example of, 104-105
play, and mental health, 11
pluripotency, defined, 121
presenilin (gene), 91
proactive interference, 36
programmed cell death, 82

reaction time, aging and, 29-31
recognition, vs. recollection, 46, 49-50
reduced initiative, in Alzheimer's disease, 21
retroactive interference, 37
rivastigmine, 90

selegiline, 87
set test, 17
short-term memory, 32
tests of, 34-35
source memory, 33
spines, of neuron, 104, 107
stem cells, 121
in adult brain, 122-123
boosting activity of, 123-124
stress
counteracting, 87-88
and dementia, 87
effects on brain, 25, 101-102

Swaab, David, 102
synapses, 26, 105

temporal lobe, 26
tests
    of creative thinking, 65, 67
    of delayed recall, 76-78
    of *Einstellung* effect, 62-65
    Jar Game, 62-65
    of memory span, 37
    of mental status, 14-15
    of paired associate learning, 41,
    43
    screening for dementia, 17
    of short-term memory, 34-35
    time and change, 16
    trail making
    of vocabulary skills, 31
    Wisconsin Card Sorting Test, 59-
    60
time and change test, 17
totipotency, defined, 121
transcranial magnetic stimulation
    (TMS), 110
transient ischemic attacks (TIAs), 80

use it or lose it model, 101, 102,
    103, 106
    childhood and, 106
    experimental evidence of, 107-
    108, 119
    importance of, 124-125

ventricles, brain, 122-123
visual working memory, 42, 46-47
vitamin C, 83
vitamin E, 81
    to combat free radical damage,
    83, 84
vocabulary skills, 31

wear and tear model, 101-102
    refutation of, 102-103
white matter, 39
Wisconsin Card Sorting Test, 59-60
working memory, 33-34

SOLUTIONS TO EXERCISES

DIGI-CLUE, page 133

Missing Number: 4

DOUBLE-UP, page 134

1. b   **2.** e   **3.** p
4. k   **5.** g   **6.** h

DIGIT-TALLY, page 135

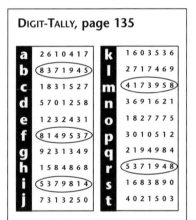

a	2 6 1 0 4 1 7	**k**	1 6 0 3 5 3 6
b	(8 3 7 1 9 4 5)	**l**	2 7 1 7 4 6 9
c	1 8 3 1 5 2 7	**m**	(4 1 7 3 9 5 8)
d	5 7 0 1 2 5 8	**n**	3 6 9 1 6 2 1
e	1 2 3 2 4 3 1	**o**	1 8 2 7 7 7 5
f	(8 1 4 9 5 3 7)	**p**	3 0 1 0 5 1 2
g	9 2 3 1 3 4 9	**q**	2 1 9 4 9 8 4
h	1 5 8 4 8 6 8	**r**	(5 3 7 1 9 4 8)
i	(5 3 7 9 8 1 4)	**s**	1 6 8 3 8 9 0
j	7 3 1 3 2 5 0	**t**	4 0 2 1 5 0 3

SPOKESAMATICIAN, page 136

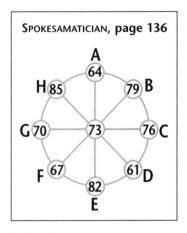

WORD WHEEL, page 138

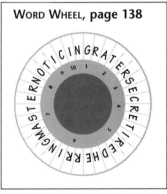

COINTEST, page 137

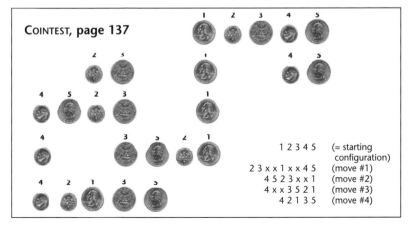

1 2 3 4 5	(= starting configuration)
2 3 x x 1 x x 4 5	(move #1)
4 5 2 3 x x 1	(move #2)
4 x x 3 5 2 1	(move #3)
4 2 1 3 5	(move #4)

Catch a New Brain Wave!

Brainwaves Books ■ 252 Great Western Road ■ South Yarmouth, MA 02664
VOICE (toll-free): 1-8778-SMARTS, ■ FAX: 508/760.2397 ■ EMAIL:<brainwaves@mediaone.net>

Recent discoveries about common mental diversities

Did you like this book? Ask your bookseller for one of these others by the same authors. They all help keep your brain interested, entertained and equipped to stick with you all your life. If your bookseller doesn't have these books, order directly from the publisher (see above). For more details, new tests and neat puzzles check *www.brainwaves.com.*

How New and Old Brains Acquire & Recall Information (January 2001)

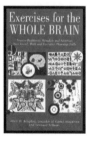

Left-Brain Conditioning Exercises and Tips to Strengthen Language, Math and Uniquely Human Skills

Conditioning Exercises for the Six Intelligence Zones

Neuron-Builders to Stimulate and Entertain Your Visual, Math and Executive-Planning Skills

Can You Pass Any of These 45 Real-Life Professional and Academic Exams?

Distribution to the book trade by I.P.G. 800/888.4741
Brainwaves® is a registered trademark of Allen D. Bragdon Publishers, Inc.